Saved by Grace, Now What?

Pam Pegram

Jesus first Pam Pegram
Matthew 6:33

RELEVANT PAGES PRESS

Table of Contents

Will Pursuing this Relationship with Jesus Mean my Life will be Easy?

Will There Ever Come a Time when I feel like I have Completed This Journey?

A Note from Pam

Hi! I am happy you have chosen this book. Are you like so many who are unsure how to walk with Jesus and make Him the center of your life? Do you fill a bit overwhelmed with it all? Me too! Whether you are a new Christian or one who has grown complacent, I am glad you are here. Regardless of where you are in your relationship with Jesus, we all need to know Him more. Together, we can do this!

My name is Pam and I am not a famous author or a biblical scholar. I am probably a lot like you. I have made my share of mistakes, experienced good times and bad, and sometimes feel inadequate, unworthy and not good enough. Yet, I long to know Jesus more! Can we walk this journey together and discover how to have an intimate relationship with our Savior?

Jesus loves us so much that He was willing to die for us. It's time we learn to live our lives for Him. Let's claim the abundant life Jesus came to offer us and find our way to an intimate relationship with our Savior. Are you ready? Let's do this!

Acknowledgments

Where do I begin? There are many who played a part in *Saved by Grace, Now What?* becoming a reality. I am forever grateful to all of you who walked this journey with me. It is your belief in this project that kept me moving forward when I wanted to give up. I will never forget your kind words, your encouragement and your unwavering faith in this book.

I cannot accept any praise for this at all. I must give credit where credit is due – this was God, y'all. I wish there was time to tell all He has done, shown me, taught me and carried me through. I wish I could explain the moments we have had. What an awesome God He is! This book is proof that He will equip the unequipped and qualify the unqualified to accomplish His will. Thank you, Lord! I love you and praise your Holy Name!

Thank you to my sweet family. Tom, I love you and am grateful for your encouragement, support, patience and servant heart during this process. Thank you for keeping me covered in prayer and pushing me when I wanted to quit. Thank you for the sacrifices you have made to make this possible. Thank you to my children, Jessica, Megan and Colby for being my biggest cheerleaders. You three inspire me and push me to be my best and to keep my eyes on Jesus. You are my greatest gifts. Thank you to my other kids (their spouses) Cam, Tyler and Hanna, for sitting in the cheer section and believing in this book. We are thankful God brought you into our family. And thank you to the most amazing parents ever. Mama and Daddy, you two love so big and serve so well. Thank you for the example you have set for us to follow and for supporting me with all your heart. Thank you to my mom, my brother, Scott and Jessica for reading and re-reading manuscripts.

To my beautiful granddaughters, Macie, Abigail and Amelia, *you inspire me to write.* I love you three more than I can put into mere words! I love our conversations about Jesus and singing praises to Him with you. It is my greatest prayer that you each will grow up to be passionate followers of Christ. You three will lead the way for our precious new additions – Hadley and Lillian – due this spring. Paw Paw, aka Boo, and I are so blessed God gave you all to us! This book is dedicated to you. May you enjoy an intimate relationship with your Savior. Put Jesus first, girls! He will never fail you.

How do I thank all who have played a role in this book becoming a reality? I love you and am forever grateful to you. Your affirmation, belief in this process and kind gestures have meant so much. There have been pivotal times when your words were exactly what God used to move me forward. Thank you to Kathy Boyd, Aimee Lamar, and Jeff and Marla

Weeks for your enthusiasm, prayers and being *all in* from the very beginning. Thank you to my pastors, Patrick and Treasa Conrad for more than I can list here. Patrick, you have taught me so much about God's word and inspired me to know Him more – therefore, creating a burden in my heart to pass that along. Treasa, thank you for teaching me to be *me* and let God use my strengths for His glory. Your support has meant the world. Mollie Sims, thank you for reaffirming the need for this book repeatedly. Your excitement for what God was calling me to do fueled my desire to walk in obedience to Him. Thank you for reading and providing fresh insight early on. Greg Belknap, you have believed in me and encouraged me every single step of the way. You have a way of keeping me focused on doing exactly what God has called me to do and not stray outside of that. Thank you, my friend. And then to Peggy Horner, there are no words. Your friendship, love and support has been such a sweet blessing. Thank you for the prayers, encouragement and guidance along the way.

Thank you to the village who came alongside me to get this project in print. These people quickly became friends and I could have never done this without them. Thank you to Stephanie and Jennifer at Relevant Pages Press for seeing the value in this book and the need it would fulfill. You have taught me much and I am forever grateful for you. Thank you to my editor, Dana. You made the process of refining painless and became a source of encouragement. Thank you to Betts for making everything look so good. You are gifted and a delight to work alongside. Thank you to the talented

Craig Callison for your patience as we eventually found our way to the perfect cover. I love it so!

Then there is my tribe! How blessed I am to have such treasured friends! You all are so special to me. Thank you for being faithful prayer partners, prodding me forward and holding my hand. You will never know the part your encouragement played in my finishing this book. You all are the best! Thank you so much to Marla, Gina, Delilah, Elissa, Allyson, Carmen, Roberta, Ginger, Kaleigh, Leigh Ann, Alyson, Emily, Paige, Alicia, Brittany, Anita, Sherry, Kim, Ashley, Jennifer, Nancy, Terri, Penny, Kiesha, Pam, Whitney, Mare, Sheila, and my manager, Gayla. (LOL!) Seriously! What would I have done without you all? I love you so much!

And to the readers of this book – whoever you may be – thank you for traveling this journey with me. I pray it blesses you and challenges you to get to know Jesus in a way you never have. I am praying you enjoy a rich, intimate relationship with your Savior! May you never be the same. All my love to you!

Chapter One
Where Am I?

Have you ever been lost? The more you try to get your bearings or find a familiar landmark, the more baffled you become. Your heart races, your hands sweat and you wonder which way you are supposed to turn. How will you get to your desired destination? Wait, forget the desired destination! How will you find your way home again? You should stop and ask for directions, but you hope the next intersection will provide new insight. Nope, you are still lost and wondering, *Where Am I?* Being lost is a terrible feeling, mixed with fear and uncertainty.

Even if you cannot recall being physically lost, we can both recount a time when we were spiritually lost. Our sin separated us from God and doomed us to hell. We were headed in the wrong direction when we realized we needed a Savior and could not go one more minute without Him. We prayed and cried out to God asking for forgiveness. We surrendered our life to Him and asked Jesus to come and be Lord of our life. As our hearts broke before Him, something wonderful happened: we felt great relief because we were no longer lost. We had been found. In that moment, we knew that we knew that we were now His and He was ours.

"Child of the King" is the greatest title we could ever obtain. It is a title we did not have to strive for, but one we simply surrendered to receive. We did not earn it and we certainly do not deserve it, yet we have received this amazing gift of eternal fellowship with our Savior. It is a wonderful feeling to know we are no longer spiritually lost. But can I be honest with you? Even though I have been saved by God's amazing grace and know I will spend eternity with Him, there have been times when I have felt really lost. Not lost, as in no longer saved, but lost as in uncertain about what it means to have a relationship with Jesus. Have you felt lost, too?

Can we agree that 'lost' is not a place we wish to be? A GPS system can help prevent us from becoming physically lost, and our salvation means we are no longer spiritually lost, but what about that lost feeling we have when it comes to growing closer to Jesus? It is our personal relationship with Him that has saved us and is also what will sustain us. So, in those times when we feel lost and long for direction, we have become relationally lost. We may have just begun our journey with Jesus and have no idea what living for him means. Or we may have accepted Him long ago, but realize we don't truly know Him. We have lost our way in our relationship with Jesus.

Not so long ago, a friend of mine shared with me that she was feeling lost. She and her husband had been living the party life, but as new parents they began to feel something was missing. Then God orchestrated a friendship with a couple who shared Jesus with them. They listened, the seed was planted and a few weeks later they prayed and asked Jesus into their hearts. The day my friend was baptized, I was standing there as she came up out of the water looking like a deer caught in the headlights. As she walked toward me, I could tell she was overwhelmed. She whispered, "Does this mean I have to be perfect?" To which I replied, "Absolutely not. This means nothing can separate you from your heavenly Father who loves you so! You have received His grace and have the Holy Spirit alive in you to do a perfecting work in you."

As we continued to chat, she revealed how lost she felt. She was not sure what to tell her friends, if she could still hang out with them, or if it was okay to drink alcohol. She was concerned she wouldn't be a good enough Christian because she knew nothing about the Bible and could not ever imagine quoting a scripture. She had all these ideas about what she believed she was supposed to do now that she was a Christian, but no idea how to implement any of them. Although she knew she had been saved and was overjoyed about that, she was feeling totally lost and longed to know how to have a close relationship with Jesus.

It is normal for a new Christian to feel a bit lost. Our salvation is just the beginning of a lifelong journey of establishing intimacy with Christ. I wish that was the only time we would ever find ourselves feeling relationally lost, but somehow we make our way there again and even again.

Sometimes it is because we have let sin in our life push Jesus away. Other times we lose our way because we are consumed with our daily life and think we are too busy to make time for Jesus. We wake up one day and realize we have lost our way and again recognize our need for intimacy with our Savior.

I have felt relationally lost more times than I care to admit. I was raised in a loving Christian home and attended Sunday School, Sunday services and Wednesday night prayer meetings. I read my Bible, went to church camp, and was active in our youth group. However, being popular was more important to me than being set apart. I followed the crowd more than I should have and lived as if being happy was what life was all about. As I look back, I realize that although I loved Jesus and had accepted Him as my personal Savior, I had not grown much past that point. I thought I knew what I needed to know, but what I needed most was to know Jesus more.

As a young adult, I thought too highly of my feelings and opinions. I would pray and spend time with the Lord, but it was all one-sided, focusing on the things I wanted and thought I needed. My need for a husband and children was top priority. I married at the ripe old age of 19 and just five years later found myself in a difficult marriage and desperately wanting God to fix it. We were young and loved Jesus, but neither of us knew how to walk with Him. I loved my husband and our two little girls, but I was miserable. I prayed, pleading for God to change my spouse; however, I honestly cannot recall asking Him to change me. There were issues that needed to be addressed, we both needed to grow up in Christ and some good solid marriage counseling was definitely in order. Instead, I expected Jesus to be like a genie in a bottle, pop out, grant my wishes and fix this failing marriage. When that did not happen, I bailed. I was left feeling disillusioned, off-course and a bit angry. I focused on my unhappiness and problems, losing sight of Jesus and His love for me.

In my wandering, I jumped into the driver's seat of my life and shortly entered my second marriage without asking God for guidance. We added baby number three, built a new house, worked hard, practically lived at the ball-field, camped, and lived what looked like a near-perfect life. The only thing missing was a deep connection to Jesus. I knew I needed Him and once again did all the things good Christian girls do: went to church, attended Bible study, taught my children about the Lord and made an effort to live for Him. Life pretty much continued that way for a dozen years or so. I took steps forward and grew closer to the Lord during that time and if you had asked me, I would have told you I had a deep, intimate relationship with Him. Looking back, I realize I was heading in the right direction, just taking the long scenic route. Instead of plugging into the Bible, God's Positioning System, I used Pam's Positioning System. I put my wants and desires before my relationship with Jesus and relied on me more than I relied on Him. It took bringing me to my breaking point to discover that like so many Christians I was relationally lost and did not even know it.

I loved my husband and our life together. Life was good

when suddenly I was blindsided and discovered my perfect life was not perfect at all. My world began to unravel and it was almost more than I could bear. I felt like I had stepped into quicksand and was spiraling downward. The gory details do not matter. The reality is I had been blissfully happy with my life and now there was going to be a second divorce leaving me a single mom of three teenagers. I was devastated. One day I "woke up" and asked, "How in the world did I get here?" I felt as if my heart had shattered into a million tiny pieces.

There I was in my own deer in the headlight moment, lost and confused, reeling in uncertainty. My marriage was disintegrating and my relationship with Jesus was completely off-track. Suddenly, I could see I had mistakenly made so many other things my saviors: my husband, my children and my work were all more important to me and came before my relationship with the One who would never leave me or forsake me. My brokenness revealed I needed to find my way back home to Jesus. He was the answer to all my questions: How would I get through this, raise my kids, find peace, have security, and go on to live an abundant life? It was time to find true intimacy with Jesus and put Him in His proper place - first.

You may be feeling lost, too. Maybe like me, you have treated Jesus like a first cousin. You love your cousin and can hardly wait to see them at Christmas and Easter. You enjoy your time together and promise to stay in touch, yet you rarely do. You intend to, but life gets in the way and another year passes. While you know her, love her and would like to say you are close, the truth is you really aren't. Can you relate that relationship to your relationship with Jesus? You know Him and love Him, yet you cannot call your relationship close. Now, you find yourself longing to experience Him and know Him more. Like my friend, you know you have been saved but what to do next is a fuzzy blur of questions about how to live and what to do. You wonder how in the world you are supposed to walk with Him.

Whether you are a new Christian or one who has lost intimacy with Jesus, can we partner up? The good news is we are not expected to figure out our route towards a relationship with Him on our own. God has it all mapped out for us; all we need to do is follow His directions. God will guide us, just like when we program our destination into our GPS. He says *"Your ears shall hear a word behind you saying, 'This is the way; walk in it.'"* [1] He will let us know what we need to do, what we need to change, and what steps we need to take. Let's get started.

We have acknowledged this place called 'lost' is not a place we wish to be and it is not where God desires for us to be either. He loved us so much He sent His son to die for us. He promised that if we believed in Him we would not perish but spend eternity with Him.[2] Because we believe this, we have accepted Jesus as our Savior. God sent His Son to offer us the hope of eternity, an example of how to live our life and so we could have a relationship with Him. Our salvation is our starting point on the path to intimacy with Jesus. As we move through the chapters in this book, we will take steps to draw closer and closer to Him.

Buckle up and get ready. This is going to be an exciting journey and I am thrilled we are traveling together. The road may not always be smooth and easy. We may encounter some speed bumps and potholes along the way, but that's okay. God has us. He knows the plans He has for us and the unique purpose each of us was created to fulfill.[3] He loves us and wants to take us on the journey of discovering oneness with Jesus, one step at a time.

A Point to Ponder

As we start this journey, let's first pull into a rest stop and take time to express our gratitude for this precious gift of salvation. It is worthy of celebration! We received a gift so great it is hard to comprehend. Because of this gift our life is new, our future is filled with hope and our eternity is secure.

Once I had an incredible opportunity to visit an inner-city church with an amazing outreach program. They were sharing the gospel with gang members, drug dealers, and people most of us would be afraid to look in the eye. I sat in awe at a table for ten and listened to a former gang member tell of the terrible things he had done when he was lost. He was burdened as he spoke of things that were inconceivable to me. He struggled as he shared about a life full of evil and despair. As he began to share how Jesus saved him, I noticed his whole demeanor changed. It was as if someone switched on a light bulb inside of him and he began to glow. His voice quivered as he talked about God's grace.

He almost shouted as he clenched his fist, pounded his chest and proclaimed, "Jesus died for me!"

As I listened, his overflowing gratitude made an impression on me. Our salvation means we will spend eternity in Heaven with our King. It means we will never have to endure hell. This brother in Christ understood hell in a way most of us never will; his life on the streets had been worse than any form of hell we could imagine. His salvation had great value to him and there are not words big enough for me to describe his gratitude. I left there that day changed.

Oh, if only our gratefulness matched the enormity of God's gift, His only Son's life for ours.

Oh, if only our gratefulness matched the enormity of God's gift, His only Son's life for ours. Jesus left the right hand of God, came to earth in human form for us, was mistreated, questioned, and mocked. He was blameless, yet chose to bear our sin and die so we could have the hope of eternity with Him. He willingly bore our shame, suffered, was severely beaten and nailed to a cross to offer us this precious gift of salvation. Because of our sin, we could never be good enough to save ourselves. Therefore, Jesus paid the penalty for our sins and *"God declares us 'not guilty' of offending Him if we trust in Jesus Christ, who in His kindness freely takes away our sins."*[4] He shed His precious blood so we could be washed white as snow. In 2 Corinthians,

Paul says, *"Thanks be to God for His indescribable gift!"*[5] God's sacrifice of His son, Jesus' willingness to die for us, and His grace truly are indescribable.

Before you turn the page...

- *Think about the gift you have been given through your salvation and express your gratitude to your Savior. Let the enormity of His gift overwhelm you.*

Chapter 2
Who Am I?

Our salvation is only the beginning of our transformation. It is our starting point on the path to intimacy with our King; the place we return to when we lose our way; and the path we are called to walk. *So now what?*

Let's begin this journey by embracing who we are, now that we are His. The Bible tells us that when we are in Christ, we are a new creation; the old has passed away and the new has come.[6] It is exciting to know we are new in Christ, that our sin has been washed away and we can now identify with Him. However, we may be feeling a lot like our old self, still struggling with the same habits, insecurities, fears, and problems. Just like before, we still find our identity in the wrong things and although we know we are a child of God, we struggle to see ourselves as He sees us. This will never change unless we exchange God's truth for the lies we have believed far too long. It is time to stop looking in all the wrong places and discover our true identity.

The problem is we live in a fallen world and it is easy

to be consumed by its trappings – beauty, wealth, and material possessions. We are surrounded by images of models and beautiful celebrities and believe our identity is defined by our appearance, so we seek to look better, be more fit, and appear younger. We think our identity is found in our outward beauty, but *it's not*. We get up every day and head off to our job. We know others who are more successful, have high-level positions and make more money. We believe our identity is found in our career or lack thereof, but *it's not*. We get on social media and we see seemingly perfect families made up of perfect marriages with perfect children all harmoniously living perfect lives. We feel our life pales in comparison. We believe our identity is gauged by our ability to create the perfect life, but *it's not*. You see, these images the world offers us are not where we are to find our identity.

Our true identity is also hidden behind the labels that have been used to falsely identify us throughout our lives, and in our ignorance, we accepted them. Maybe we were called names as children and those names became labels that stuck: bad, unruly, difficult, mistake, ugly, fat, or others. We go through life and bad things happen to us, layering on the unwanted labels of abused, unwanted, divorced, rejected, bitter, angry, desperate, lonely, damaged, guilty, and others far worse. Then we compare ourselves with others and create our own labels, such as failure, not good enough, stupid, unworthy, unlovable, and so many more. Just reading those words stirs up emotions in us and some of them cause us to feel a twinge of pain. Would you take a few minutes and circle the labels that resonate with you? If your labels are not listed, jot them in the margin of this page; it will only take a minute.

Now, look back at the words you circled and the words you have written. These words are labels you wear every day just as you would wear a name tag to a meeting. These harsh words are *not* who you are; they are lies. The truth, the only truth, in this fallen world we live in is God's truth. You can scour the Bible over and over again and God will never place any of these labels on you. It is time to rip these labels off, wad them up and discard them with the trash for they are rubbish! It is time for you to know and embrace your true identity.

When we wear the wrong set of labels, we lose sight of who we really are. First, we must understand we have been created with worth and value. These have been instilled in us by our Creator and nothing we have done or said, no terrible act we have committed, nothing that has ever happened to us and no words that have ever been spoken to us have diminished our value, not one little bit. We are who God says we are. He breathed life into us, filling us with His purpose, His worth and His value. Do you accept that or are you still having a hard time grasping it?

I remember a time when I was broken and had lost my sense of identity. I was at a meeting where the speaker took out a $100 bill. He held it up and asked the crowd to shout out the value of the bill. Everyone replied in unison, "$100." He began to talk about things that happen in our life. As he spoke he wadded the bill up, threw it on the ground

> *Our value, worth, and the love our Creator has for us stays intact no matter what we endure or what we do.*

and stomped on it with his shoe, symbolizing the damage we incur in our life. At the end of the demonstration he picked up the bill, straightened it out and smoothed it with his hand. He held up the now crumpled, dirty and damaged $100 bill and again asked the crowd to shout out its value. Again, everyone replied in unison, "$100." As tears streamed down my cheeks and splashed on my notepad, I realized our value, worth, and the love our Creator has for us stays intact no matter what we endure or what we do. God's love is unconditional and He sees great value in us.

The evil one started spreading his lies way back in the Garden of Eden and today we are still listening. When Adam and Eve sinned, they picked up the baggage of shame and regret, trying to hide under their fig leaves. But remember what happened? They foolishly thought God couldn't see them, but of course He could. God knows all. So why are we hiding? Our fig leaves are no longer needed because God already knows what we have done, said, and even thought. When we carry this same baggage, we allow Satan to steal our identity from us. It is the original identity theft and believe me, this type of identity theft has much harsher repercussions than someone stealing your Social Security number.

We don't need to drag around our baggage - God sent His Son to set us free. We can set these burdens at the foot of the cross and leave them there. The Bible tells us that God daily bears our burdens and frees us.[7] But we must let go of them, stop looking back and start looking forward so we can become who God created us to be.

We have talked about who we are not, we have learned we have worth and value, and we are trying to pry our hands off our baggage, but we need to know who we are. Who better to ask than the One who made us? If anyone knows who we are, wouldn't you agree it is the only One who knows everything about us? He loves us so much He wrote our identity in His word so that anytime we forget, we can rediscover our truth. Let's jump into God's word to see what labels He says we are to wear today and every day.

God tells us in His word that because we have believed in Him and received Him, we have the right to be called a *Child of God*.[8] You, my friend, are a *Child of The King*! I hope this label excites you and makes your heart race just a bit. Because of what He did, we are *Redeemed* and *Forgiven*.[9] How do you like those labels? *Redeemed* means we have been bought back - a ransom has been paid for us, therefore confirming God finds value in us. Because Jesus paid the price for our sins, we are forgiven, no longer guilty. We are forgiven, therefore *Blameless* – no need for shame.

We have been *Chosen*,[10] therefore we can know we are *Wanted*. The Creator of the Universe has *chosen* us and *wants* us. Because of His great love for us, He sent His Son so we could have a relationship with Him. Jesus has

> *God gave us a soulmate when He sent Jesus to die for our sins.*

initiated a relationship with us and is waiting for us to grow that relationship into a deep friendship.

God tells us we are **Complete**[11] in Him and no longer need to look for someone to complete us. The world tells us we need a soulmate, but God gave us a soulmate when He sent Jesus to die for our sins. He is all we need and the only One who will truly satisfy us. He wants to be our soulmate, best friend and constant companion.

We are more than **Conquerors**.[12] Regardless of what we face we can trust God and depend on Him. We are promised He will never leave us and will use our trials for good in our lives.

God's calls us His **Masterpiece**, His **Creation**.[13] I have heard Andy Horner, one of my spiritual mentors, say many times, "God didn't take time to make any junk." You know what? I believe that. *Do you?* We are **Loved**,[14] but not just a little. He has lavished His love on us. The world teaches us to love those who love us, but that is easy. God loves those who do not love Him, those who mock Him, those who disobey Him. He loved us long before we made the decision to love Him. That is awe-inspiring. Would you suffer for someone who would not even give you the time of day? We are **Loved** with an unconditional love greater than we can comprehend. As His beloved child, we are His **Heir**[15] and will inherit His kingdom. Therefore, we are **Secure**.[16]

Anytime you struggle with your identity, study the scriptures linked to these labels and know your identity is found in who God is and what He has done. He is not concerned with our past; it is forgotten. He is only concerned with who we are becoming. Don't waste time looking backwards, struggling with your past. Let it go and move forward, focusing on getting to know Jesus in a much deeper way.

Are you thinking letting go is easier said than done? I promised I would be real with you, so here I go. I know who God says I am. I have studied His word and written down His description of me in detail. I wear the right set of labels most days. But some days I hear Satan hiss and I find myself going back and digging one or two of those false labels out of the trash. The adhesive on those things is incredible; they stick without any problem. Why do we do that? Why do we listen to the world instead of listening to the One who created us and the One who died for us? Why do we discard God's truth so easily and buy into the devil's lies that only bring about pain and destruction? Well, the only answer is unbelief. We battle with unbelief.

Unbelief is as old as sin, *literally.* Adam and Eve doubted they were enough and wanted what Satan hissed about. Like them, our unbelief will rob us of our true identity if we allow it. It is a hidden sin that we do not even realize stands between us and God and thwarts our attempts to embrace who God says we are. We need to address our unbelief, *but how*?

There is a story in the book of Mark about a father who brought his son to Jesus for healing. The boy had several problems, one being that he was possessed by a demon that kept him from speaking and caused him to have seizures. The boy's father cried out and asked Jesus to help him. Jesus replied,

> *"If you can believe, all things are possible to him who believes." Immediately the father of the child cried out and said with tears, "Lord, I believe; help my unbelief!"*[17]

So, there is our answer. Even though we say we believe what the Bible says, we are harassed by our doubting thoughts, our unbelief about who God says we are. We only need to ask Jesus to help us with our unbelief.

Jesus tells us,

> *The thief does not come except to steal, and to kill, and to destroy. I have come that they may have life, and that they may have it more abundantly.*[18]

So what are we going to choose? Identity theft or abundant life? Satan's lies or God's truth? No more letting Satan steal our identity, no more listening to His lies or our negative self-talk. Instead, we can saturate our mind with God's word, talk to ourselves about who He says we are and **believe it**!

Something to Do

- When we write something down, it is more likely to stick with us. Will you take a few minutes and write down the labels God wants you to wear? Write them in this book or on a piece of paper you can hang on the fridge. Doodle them in pretty colors.

- Grab your Bible and highlight the scriptures listed in this chapter.

Don't forget the precious words God has spoken about YOU.

Chapter 3
What Is Mine?

Are you wearing your tiara today? It can feel a bit intimidating to accept that we are a member of the royal family. But regardless of whether we feel worthy or not, we *are* a Daughter of the King. When we accepted Jesus as our Savior, our adoption was finalized, our redemption sealed, and our place in the castle secured. Although Jesus is the only natural Son, God has graciously adopted us and made us His. We have received all rights and privileges bestowed onto any heir to His throne.

A friend of mine has twin granddaughters who her daughter gave up for adoption at birth. God made a way, during a very difficult situation, to protect and provide for these girls. The couple who adopted them openly accepted the birth mom and her family and have allowed them to be a part of their lives. It is a beautiful story of grace, redemption and unconditional love. As I scroll through the pictures posted and listen to their stories, there is no evidence these two beautiful little girls have no biological connection to the mom and dad who adopted them. In every way, they are theirs. These girls, innocent and carefree, have no idea what a gift they have been given.

The same is true in our story - our beautiful story of grace, redemption and unconditional love. You see, we began as slaves to our sin, but God sent Jesus to pay the price for those sins and purchase us out of slavery. His death on the cross offered us freedom and cleared the way for us to become Daughters. God graciously adopted us and made us His.[19] As an heir, we will receive an inheritance that far exceeds any worldly goods. Our inheritance offers us His presence, His provision and His promises.

His Presence...

We have been given the right to enter His presence, to have a relationship with Him and to grow intimate with our King. Think about that. Has there ever been an earthly king, a president, a corporate executive who would allow us that level of access to them? No! Even if we could get in the door, we would be required to have an appointment. But here is the Creator of the Universe offering us the privilege of fellowship with Him. He is our "Abba Father"[20] and has made His home with us. Jesus said, *"If anyone loves Me, he will keep My word; and My Father will love him, and We will come to him and make Our home with him."*[21]

God sent His Son Jesus so we could have a relationship with Him. We are to develop a deep fellowship by spending time in His presence. We might think that if He were physically here with us, it would be easier to sit and chat and ask questions. If that was the case, our time with Him would be limited by availability and location. God had a better plan. When the time was nearing for Christ to be crucified, He told His disciples it was to their advantage for Him to go away because God was sending someone in His place.[22] He was referring to the Holy Spirit. He told them that although He could not be everywhere with each of them, the Holy Spirit would be. The Holy Spirit indwelled us the minute we surrendered our heart to Jesus. He is alive in us. We will talk in detail in the next chapter about the Trinity – God the Father, the Son and the Holy Spirit – but today rest in the fact that we can experience them in a real way.

God offers us His presence because He loves us. His word tells us His love is unconditional and everlasting. All we need to do is accept that truth and love Him in return. It is our love for Him that will lead us to walk in obedience to Him, and it is our obedience to Him that allows us to fellowship with Him. David said in Psalm 16:11,

> You will show me the path of life; in Your presence is fullness of joy; at Your right hand are pleasures forevermore.

> *It is our love for Him that will lead us to walk in obedience to Him, and it is our obedience to Him that allows us to fellowship with Him.*

As we continue together, let's find joy in the journey and be open to experience God and everything He has for us.

His Provision...

As heirs, we are recipients of God's provision. He tells us that if He feeds the birds, how much more will He do for us?[23] So much of what He does and has done we don't see or, at the very least, we take for granted. The breath in our lungs, our ability to see the words on these pages, and the people around us are all part of God's provision for us. We have so much to be thankful for, yet we spend very little time thanking Him. God's word tells us that *"Every good gift and every perfect gift is from above and comes down from the Father..."*[24] and that He will *"supply all your needs according to His riches in glory by Christ Jesus."*[25]

While we may not have all we want or we foolishly think we need, God will care for us and supply what we need if we trust in Him. In Matthew 6:31-33 Jesus tells us,

> *Therefore, do not worry, saying, 'What shall we eat?' or 'What shall we drink?' or 'What shall we wear?' For after all these things the Gentiles seek. For your heavenly Father knows that you need all these things. But seek first the kingdom of God and His righteousness, and all these things shall be added to you.*

When we learn to seek Him first, we develop our faith and learn to truly trust in Him for everything.

His provision for us is abundant. As we grow in our intimacy with Jesus, we will come to see that He is all we need. We have a list of what we call needs that are merely wants. God knows best and has already laid a plan to provide for us. We just need to learn to walk in faith, to trust in Him and to surrender our way in exchange for His way. To help us, He has provided some pretty incredible promises.

His Promises...

As children of God, every promise in the Bible is ours. We read God's word and think He is offering those wonderful promises to the holy, good and perfect people. But because we are His, His promises are ours. There are hundreds of promises, maybe even thousands, I'm not certain. But, I am certain He wants you to believe His word and learn to trust in what He has promised.

> *Because we are His, His promises are ours.*

Many people are afraid to surrender their life to Christ because they fear what they will be required to give up and what rules they will have to follow. But the truth is when we surrender our all to Jesus, what we get in return is more than we could have ever imagined. Check out these promises:

Therefore, if anyone is in Christ, he is a new creation; old things have passed away; behold, all things have become new. 2 Corinthians 5:17

God promised us new life in Christ. As we study God's word we learn we can walk in newness in Him.[26] We grow and change and break free from our fears, insecurities, habits, regrets, hurts, and baggage that enslave us. We learn His way offers us freedom – the freedom required to become who He created us to be.

> *"For I know the plans I have for you," declares the Lord, "plans to prosper you and not to harm you, plans to give you hope and a future."* Jeremiah 29:11

God has a plan and a specific purpose for each of us being here and it is good. He has promised us hope and a secure future.

> *And we know that all things work together for good to those who love God, to those who are called according to His purpose.* Romans 8:28

God promises good will come from every trial and heartbreak. He can use these times to teach us to trust Him, to grow our faith in Him and to ignite our passion for Him. This is where we learn the meaning of Genesis 50:20 - *"But as for you, you meant evil against me, but God meant it for good."* You see, no matter what evil comes our way, God will work His good plan.

I love this quote, "In a thousand trials, it is not just five hundred of them that work for the good of the believer, but nine hundred and ninety-nine, plus one." George Mueller

Be anxious for nothing, but in everything by prayer and supplication, with thanksgiving, let your requests be made known to God; and the peace of God, which surpasses all understanding, will guard your hearts and minds through Christ Jesus. Philippians 4:6-7

Worry is worthless, a complete waste of our time that changes nothing and robs us of peace. We are to bring our requests to God through prayer, asking Him to guide, protect and carry us. Our faith allows us to leave that request and trust Him with the outcome.

For some, anxiety can be debilitating and may require professional help. For others, it is just a case of learning to surrender our old ways and choosing to believe God is bigger than our circumstances. There may be times when you pray and lay a burden down, giving it to God, only to pick it back up minutes later. Pray and lay it down again, however many times it takes, until you learn to leave it there and trust God with it. By doing this, you will be able to experience the peace that can only come from God.

Fear not, for I am with you; be not dismayed, for I am your God. I will strengthen you. Yes, I will help you. I will uphold you with My righteous right hand. Isaiah 41:10

Did you know there are 365 scriptures in the Bible that tell us to not fear? That is one reminder for each day of the year. Do you think that is a coincidence? There are so many aspects of fear, from the fear of speaking in public to the fear of failing to the fear of devastation or loss. No matter – God does not want us to live with a spirit of fear. He is sovereign, preeminent in power and authority. The antidote to fear is complete and total trust in God. The more we come to know Him, the more we trust Him and the more we will have freedom from fear.

> *Have you not known? Have you not heard? The everlasting God, the Lord, the Creator of the ends of the earth, never faints or is weary. His understanding is unsearchable. He gives power to the weak, and to those who have no might He increases strength. Even the youths shall faint and be weary, and the young men shall utterly fall, but those who wait on the Lord shall renew their strength. They shall mount up with wings like eagles, they shall run and not be weary, they shall walk and not faint.* Isaiah 41:28-31

Oh, how I love this scripture! I love God's rhetorical questions. It is as if He is asking, *how could you not know this?* God is powerful and mighty and takes care of His people. When we wait, placing our confident expectation in Him, we receive a spiritual transformation and experience His power, strength and endurance.

Can I tell you something? God gave me this verse after my second divorce when I was broken, lost and in such dire need of Him. Looking back, I can now see how faithful He was to activate His power inside of me and renew me in His strength. I could walk forward in faith in Him as he restored me and planted me on the path He had prepared for me so that I could run the race He chose for me. These verses are for you, too! Are you ready to mount up on wings as eagles, to run and not be weary and to walk and not faint?

My sheep hear My voice, and I know them, and they follow Me. And I give them eternal life, and they shall never perish; neither shall anyone snatch them out of My hand. My Father, who has given them to Me, is greater than all; and no one is able to snatch them out of My Father's hand. John 10:27-29

We are His sheep and we have been promised eternal life with Him. The thought of eternity is hard to grasp, yet it is a reality and it is ours. We can know we are secure and no one can snatch us out of God's hand. He is more powerful than our enemy, therefore, we are His forevermore.

In my Father's house there are many mansions; if it were not so, I would have told you. I go to prepare a place for you. And if I go and prepare a place for you, I will come again and receive you to Myself; that where I am, there you may be also. John 14:2-3

Jesus has promised he has prepared an eternal home for us and is coming back to take us there. Oh, what a joyous day that will be! My small mind cannot even begin to fathom what it will be like to be in the physical presence of

Jesus, our Savior, the King of Kings.

Are you excited about your inheritance? Because of our salvation we have received the ability to experience God's presence; we are partakers of His divine provision, and His *exceedingly great and precious promises* are ours.[27] He has prepared the way for us. Now, let's go walk in it.

Putting it All Together

Let's review. We established our salvation is our starting point - as well as our re-starting point should we lose our way on our journey to intimacy with Jesus. We now know our true identity and have reviewed our inheritance as the adopted Daughters of God. Let's close by thanking Him for all He has given us.

Father God, thank you for the great gift we have received through our salvation. We are in awe of your almighty power and your great love for us. We rejoice in your presence and are thankful for your provision. God, we rest in Your precious promises. We are thankful You have made us a new creation and instilled a plan and a purpose for our life. We trust that everything we go through and the challenges ahead will be used to draw us closer to You and for You to receive the glory. We offer up our needs to You and lay down our anxiety so we may receive the sweet essence of your peace. We will no longer be held in bondage to fear. God, we want to experience renewal and restoration so we can be free in You. We wait on you Lord, to strengthen us and sustain us. We are secure in You and can hardly wait until Jesus returns and we spend eternity with You. In the meantime, help us Lord to grow in our relationship with Jesus. Help us to know Him in a way we have never experienced. As we get to know Him, help us to reflect Him and become more and more like Him. We love You, thank You and praise You! It is in the precious name of Jesus we pray, Amen.

Chapter 4
Who is He?

Sometimes we get caught up in the mystery of it all. There are some questions we will simply not know the answer to until we stand face to face with our Creator. Matter of fact, God is not a puzzle or a riddle we are to solve. Instead, this mystery is the consummation of God's plan through Jesus and what He has done for us. We as humans think we need to have it all make sense – yet our small minds simply can't comprehend the totality of it all.

For instance, we struggle to completely understand the Trinity. Are you thinking 'the what?' Maybe you know what it is, yet find it confusing. That's okay. It is probably the most confusing aspect of Christianity. It is hard to understand and hard to explain. Before I give it a try, let me offer a disclaimer. By now you realize I am a simple girl who loves Jesus, but not a biblical scholar. This explanation is based on my understanding and I am sure can be refuted as not exact by those more educated. However, as my daddy always said, 'Sometimes you can be too big for your britches," and think you are smarter than you are. Therefore, it is always best to base what we believe on what God says, not what any man says, educated or not. Here goes…

Throughout scripture it is clear God is both one and three. The Trinity is one God existing in three persons. There is God the Father, God the Son and God the Holy Spirit. When I was a child my mom explained it to me this way. She held up an egg and explained it was one egg – but there are three parts. There is a shell, a yolk, and an egg white. Three parts make up one egg. Our one true God is made up of three persons – each a distinct person of the Godhead. The Bible teaches that the Father is God, Jesus is God, and the Holy Spirit is God. But the Bible makes it clear there is only one God. He is our father, He is our friend, and He dwells within us to lead, guide and direct us in our daily life. Don't worry if you do not totally understand how He works. I don't totally get it either because as God tells us, *"…My ways are higher than your ways, and My thoughts than your thoughts."*[28] We will never fully understand everything on this side of Heaven. But if the Bible - God's word - says it, we can believe it to be true.

God the Father

God is the Supreme Being, the Creator of All, the Infinite One. In Revelations 1:8 we read God's self-description, *"I am the Alpha and the Omega, the Beginning and the End, says the Lord, who is and who was and who is to come, the*

Almighty." Need I say more? He is everything – the Beginning and the End and everything in between. That pretty much tells us all we need to know about who God is, right? But, just in case you want more, He is eternal and immortal,[29] incomparable,[30] and unchanging.[31]

He is our Father and is the epitome of what a good father is. He is loving,[32] truthful,[33] compassionate,[34] merciful[35] and offers grace upon grace.[36] He is holy[37] and just.[38] Because He loves us, He disciplines His children[39] and offers us redemption.[40]

When my children were teenagers I questioned why they would listen to their peers instead of listening to me. I loved them and wanted the best for them. My advice came from a place of wisdom and experience, yet at times they allowed the influence of their peers to matter more than mine. We as Christians do the same thing. Why on earth would we listen to those around us and allow this lost, fallen and broken world to have influence in our lives? We have a heavenly Father who loves us more than we can fathom and knows what is best for us.

God the Father is the ultimate source of all and has made a way for you to know Him.

God the Son

Jesus, the Son of God, is God. Confusing? Yes, it is confusing, but our inability to completely wrap our mind around it does not change the fact that it is the absolute truth. John 1:1 tells us, *"In the beginning was the Word, and* the Word was with God, and the Word was God." John uses Word to refer to Jesus Christ and this scripture declares His deity. Verse 2 goes on to tell us that like God, Jesus has always been. John 1:14 explains,

> *And The Word became flesh and dwelt among us, and we beheld His glory, the glory as of the only begotten of the Father, full of grace and love.*

Why did He come? Because

> *In this is love, not that we loved God, but that He loved us and sent His Son to be the propitiation for our sins."*[41]

Wow! God loves *us* so much He sent His Son to die for us so we could spend eternity with Him. Jesus said in John 14:6, *"I am the way, the truth, and the life. No one comes to the Father except through Me."* So, through Jesus we have forgiveness,[42] reconciliation to God[43] and have been granted eternal life.[44]

But there is more. Jesus is our friend.[45] He loves us more than anyone else loves us and lived His time on earth as an example for us to follow. He loved us enough to take on our shame and die for us.

Jesus is the King of Kings, the Lord of Lords.[46] He is the Light of the World,[47] the Rock of Salvation,[48] and the Anchor for our Soul.[49] He is the Lamb of God[50] and poured out His blood for us. He is our hope and the answer to our problems.

Even if we don't know it yet - Jesus is, can be, wants to be and will always be our very best friend. We will talk more about Him, but first, let's learn about the Holy Spirit and the important role He plays in our journey to intimacy with Jesus.

> *Jesus is, can be, wants to be, and will always be our very best friend.*

God the Holy Spirit

The Holy Spirit is God, the third person of the Trinity. The Bible tells us that when we pray to receive Jesus, the Holy Spirit indwells us and gives us the assurance of salvation. With all the science fiction movies and TV shows we are exposed to, we might be tempted to think of the Holy Spirit as a mystical being. However, He is a person who resides within believers and He is God - therefore, He is God in us. The proof of our salvation and our promise of eternal life rests on the evidence of the Holy Spirit dwelling in us, the seal of promise on our hearts[51] until the day of Jesus' return.

In John 14:26 Jesus told the disciples,

...the Helper, the Holy Spirit, whom the Father will send in My name, He will teach you all things, and bring to your remembrance all things that I said to you.

God sent this Helper to us and He is always with us.[52] Let's talk about the ways He helps us.

The Holy Spirit is the Spirit of Truth and guides us in the truth.[53] As Christians, we should base what we believe on God's word and not on the ways of the world. The Holy Spirit helps us discern what is true, just, and the will of God. He is the filter to run every decision, thought, and action through to help us to strain out the impurities and become more like Christ. The Holy Spirit is here to lead us in the ways of the Lord; our job is to follow.

The Holy Spirit is our teacher. None of us has God's wisdom and can only tap into it through the help of the Holy Spirit no matter how educated or intellectual we may be. The Helper is our interpreter, or you might say our CliffsNotes. With His help, we will grow in wisdom[54] and gain insight as we grow in our relationship with Jesus. We will begin to see things differently than the world sees it.

The Holy Spirit is also our counselor - leading us, prompting us and revealing God's will to us.[55] He shines a light on our sin, pointing it out so we can eliminate it. He never condemns us, instead He reveals our sin and encourages us to turn from it. Some of our sin is morally unacceptable by our friends and family and we know we should not do those things. Other sin is accepted by the world. The Holy Spirit helps us to discern those sins as well and turn from them. It is only when we are open to this introspection that we can change, mature and grow in our relationship with Jesus.

In addition to all of this, the Holy Spirit helps us

develop *fruit* in our life. Jesus often spoke in parables to help us better understand. He used fruit as an analogy to clarify what will bloom in our life if we live for Him. Plants do not bear fruit instantaneously and neither will we. There is a process of growing, pruning, and cleansing that must be completed before the fruits of the Spirit will be produced in our life. By abiding in Christ and lovingly obeying the Word of God, we will bear the fruits of the Spirit.

These fruits are love, joy, peace, patience, kindness, goodness, faithfulness, gentleness and self-control.[56] These qualities set us apart from this world. It is only when these fruits become evident in our life that others will let us share Jesus with them. If others look at you and see joy, love and peace in your life, that you are kind and good-hearted, walk in faith and are gentle in spirit and have self-control, they will see Jesus in you. They will see proof you are His and He is yours. They will want what you have.

My favorite scripture about the Holy Spirit is Romans 8:26-27,

Likewise the Spirit also helps in our weaknesses. For we do not know what we should pray for as we ought, but the Spirit Himself makes intercession for us with groanings which cannot be uttered. Now He who searches the hearts knows what the mind of the Spirit is, because He makes intercession for the saints according to the will of God.

Even when we do not know how to pray or what to say in

our prayers, the Holy Spirit intervenes for us. He prays for us with groanings. No language necessary because after all He is God. What a sweet gift our Father has given to us; He prays for us with groanings.

So, there we have it. God has given us Himself as our heavenly Father, His Son as our Best Friend and the Holy Spirit as our Helper. These three distinct persons of the Godhead equals our One True God. While our infinite God could never be fully described or understood, my prayer for you is that you recognize He is awesome, He is worthy of our praise and wants to be first in our life.

Something to Ponder

"As God is exalted to the right place in our lives, a thousand problems are solved all at once." A.W. Tozer

Today ask yourself, "If I put God (the Father, the Son and the Holy Spirit) first in my life, what problems would be solved? List all one thousand here. (Just kidding.) But seriously, many things would change. Think about it.

Chapter 5
Relationship vs. Practicing Religion?

How are you doing so far? We talked about our salvation and discussed who God is and who we are in Him. So now, let's start digging a little deeper and talk about the difference between practicing religion and developing a relationship with Jesus. You see, we can get confused. We are list makers, rule followers, planners and goal setters. We want a set of steps to take to achieve our goals and get to where we want to go in life by charting our own course and making our own way. We want to earn our way to Heaven, earn favor with God and even earn His love. Have we not learned anything at all?

Do you think we long to do the right things and behave the right way because we know we are unworthy? No matter how good we are, we could never earn God's love and amazing grace. So we try harder to obey the commandments and deem ourselves approved for a future in Heaven.

We go to church most Sundays, pray occasionally, read our Bible every now and then, tithe when we can, sing the hymns we like, donate what we don't want to charity, sponsor a child, etc. However, doing these things out of obligation or because we believe it is what is expected of us is simply us *practicing religion.*

Religion is man-made. It is a set of rules we follow and actions we take if we are to call ourselves religious. Practicing religion causes us to look around to see how other Christians behave. Then we simply copy their actions and believe we are religious too. If they raise their hands in praise, we raise our hands. If they kneel to pray, we kneel. We copy and do what we believe is expected.

Practicing religion can fool us into believing we have a relationship with Jesus and can give us the illusion we are growing. We may be growing more religious, but that is not the goal, is it? Theologian Karl Rahner said, "The number one cause of atheism is Christians. Those who proclaim God with their mouths and deny Him with their lifestyles is what an unbelieving world finds simply unbelievable."

Religion is dangerous business because it stifles the Holy Spirit and makes God more an enigma than a beloved Heavenly Father. It leaves no room for questions and causes us to believe that listening to a sermon is enough and there is no need to study the Bible on our own. It encourages us to put our pastors, elders, and the great men of the Bible on a pedestal, believing God could not use *us* the way He uses them. It encourages us to place our faith in our works instead of God's grace. It causes us to lie to ourselves and distracts us from the truth. Satan loves religion.

Religion focuses on our appearance. Not our physical appearance, but how we appear to be. We may appear to be religious, but God is concerned with the condition of our heart. In Matthew 23:25-28, Jesus is speaking to legalistic rule followers who valued their own guidelines and regulations more than they did the Word of God. He called them hypocrites and went on to say,

> *For you cleanse the outside of the cup and dish, but inside they are full of extortion and self-indulgence. Blind Pharisee, first cleanse the inside of the cup and dish, that the outside of them may be clean also... For you are like whitewashed tombs which indeed appear beautiful outwardly, but inside are full of dead men's bones and all uncleanness. Even so you also outwardly appear righteous to men, but inside you are full of hypocrisy and lawlessness.*

God is not calling us to clean up our outward appearance, pretend to be something we are not, or to *act* like we love Him. He is not asking us to be legalistic and think we are better than others. No, God is inviting us to have a *personal* relationship with Him through His son Jesus, who is the Way, the Truth and the Life. We are not grandfathered in because our mom or grandparents lived for Him or because we have attended the same church since we were born. He is calling us to transform from the inside out, and that can only take place as we grow to know Jesus

> *He is calling us to transform from the inside out, and that can only take place as we grow to know Jesus more and more personally.*

more and more *personally.*

I believe we practice religion because we want to know Jesus, but aren't willing to do what it takes to know Him. It is the same as with other things in our lives. We want to be fit, but are not willing to eat healthy and exercise. We want a higher paying job, but are not willing to go back to college or work our way up. We want success, but we would rather watch TV than make the sacrifices success requires. We want this fabulous relationship with Jesus, but rationalize that we are too busy to spend time with Him.

So how does a relationship with Jesus differ from religion? A relationship is defined as a significant connection between people and their involvement with one another. Asking Jesus into our heart opened the door to this incredible, life-changing, transformational connection. He *knows you* – it's time to get to know Him.

A deep connection with Jesus requires the same things required for a deep connection with anyone – love for one another, spending time together, honest communication, authenticity, trust and commitment. The fact that you are reading these pages tells me you are willing to invest time in this relationship. Spending time with Jesus must be a priority and as with any relationship, if we don't schedule it, it is not going to happen. So, make time to hang out with the King of Kings and Lord of Lords. You need this time together so He can truly become *your* King and *your* Lord.

Having a relationship with Jesus means He is a part of our daily life. In the next chapter, we will discuss action steps to take – spending time in God's word, spending time in prayer and fellowshipping with other believers. But remember, it is not going through the motions that grows our relationship with Jesus. It is investing time studying God's word the way you would listen to a friend talk; it is praying the way you would pour out your heart to your best friend; and it is taking time to gather with mutual friends so through them you will come to know Him even more. It is Relationship Building 101.

We will feel our relationship with Jesus going deeper as we learn to put Him first in our life. First does not mean a close second; *first means first.* It's not easy; as a matter of fact, it is quite a struggle. It is much easier to put our children, our mate, our career, or our selfish ways in first place. Jesus tells us we cannot serve two masters.[57] He is to come first and be our only Master. Oh, but we are tempted every day to love the world. There are things that please us,

> *We will feel our relationship with Jesus going deeper as we learn to put Him first in our life.*

make us feel good about ourselves and bring us what we believe is satisfaction – even if temporary. But God says in 1 John 2:15-17,

> *Do not love the world or the things in the world. If anyone loves the world, the love of the Father is not in him. For all that is in the world – the lust of the flesh, the lust of the eyes, and the pride of life – is not of the Father but is of the world. And the world is passing away, and the lust of it; but he who does the will of God abides forever.*

The lust of the flesh refers to our desire for sinful, sensual pleasure. The lust of the eyes refers to covetousness and materialism. The pride of life refers to being proud about one's position in the world. None of this will ever be enough to truly satisfy us and will all pass away. A relationship with Jesus is the only thing that will satiate our needs and last through eternity. It is the most important relationship, asset, possession, and position we have. We should treat it as such.

So, if we are to have an intimate relationship with Jesus, what does He want from us? He was asked to name the greatest commandment and He answered,

> *'You shall love the Lord your God with all your heart, with all your soul, and with all your mind.' This is the first and great commandment. And the second is like it: 'You shall love your neighbor as yourself.'*[58]

So, how are we doing? Scriptures tell us others will recognize us as a Christian not by our knowledge of the Bible, not by our religious affiliations, and not by our eloquent prayers. He says others will know we love Jesus by our deeds of love for one another.[59] So, what does it reveal about us when we lash out in anger, gossip, judge others, or are filled with resentment? It tells us we have a "heart" problem and need a little more transforming. You will find the more time you spend with Jesus, the more you will grow to know Him, the more you will fall in love with Him and the more love and grace you will have for others.

Since Jesus knows our innermost thoughts, fears, hurts, weaknesses, and everything about us, we have some catching up to do. We can begin to discover who Jesus is by opening our Bible and reading about Him. You see, the more we get into God's word, the more it gets into us. You might start getting to know who Jesus is by reading all the red words in the New Testament. These are the words Jesus spoke and we can learn about Him as we read what He had to say. Study the four gospels – Matthew, Mark, Luke and John - all telling the same story, just from different perspectives. It's an incredible story, the greatest love story ever written.

Trust is an important element in any relationship. When we meet someone and start getting to know them we wonder *can we trust them, will they be here for us, can we talk openly with them, will they love us even if we mess up?* Reading the gospels, you will find the answer to these questions. Getting to know Jesus helps us digest what He has done for us. The depths of His love and the agony of His suffering is proof we can trust Him. The more we trust Him, the more we will grow into someone He can trust.

Lastly, as with any relationship, there may be times when you feel distance between you and Jesus. Maybe you are not feeling His presence the way you did at one point. This is not uncommon because there is so much that distracts us in this crazy world. We only need to go back to where we established that closeness to Jesus in the first place. We can begin by acknowledging who Jesus is and putting our trust back in Him. We need to tell Him we want to know Him better. We need to ask for forgiveness for our sins, including the sin of being distracted from Him. Before we know it, we will re-establish that closeness and deep connection. Once you experience it, you know there is nothing else like it.

Do you see the difference between practicing religion and building a relationship with Christ? Practicing religion can be a laborious task, but fulfilling the great commandment to love God with all our heart, soul, and mind offers us a glorious privilege. As our relationship with Jesus grows, so does our desire to be in church, to pray, to read and study our Bible, to tithe and give back to the One who has given us

> *Practicing religion can be a laborious task, but fulfilling the great commandment to love God with all our heart, soul, and mind offers us a glorious privilege.*

so much, to sing our praise to Him and to walk in obedience to Him. Because we love Jesus, we want to fulfill His desires for us. This is not religion; this is a real, loving relationship.

Jesus is offering us an opportunity to live the abundant life. He came to give, not to get something from us. He wants us to have a life that is meaningful and purposeful. He wants us to experience joy and peace and rest in Him. He is offering us a life focused on honoring and glorifying the One who set this world in motion. I don't know about you, *but count me in*! That is what I want! Let's live for our Savior and not for this dying and wicked world. Let's get to know Jesus by opening our heart and letting down our walls. Let's fall madly in love with Him and do what it takes to build this relationship.

Do you know that no matter where you are in your relationship with Jesus, there is more? If this is a new relationship for you, you are going to love getting to know your Savior and falling in love with Him. And if you have already established a deep and abiding relationship with your King, you are going to be amazed to discover there is still more. He offers us spiritual abundance in Him.

The rest of our lives should be spent striving to know Jesus more and more. In 2 Peter 3:18 we read,

> *You therefore, beloved, since you know this beforehand, beware lest you also fall from your own steadfastness, being led away with the error of the wicked; but grow in the grace and knowledge of our Lord and Savior Jesus Christ.*

It's a battle to stay the course. We will grow and then lose our way, practice religion and then reconnect our relationship, mature and then become distracted. But one day we will know Him as we are known. Can you imagine? I Corinthians 13:12 says,

For now we see in a mirror, dimly, but then face to face. Now I know in part, but then I shall know just as I also am known.

Oh, my friend, Jesus is good. His love endures forever. He is all we need, our everything, our best friend. He is our one and only, our true soul mate. When we put Him first in our life, love Him with all our heart, soul and mind, spend time with Him daily and follow the example He left for us we will be satisfied, complete, content and whole. Once we come to understand that and live as if we believe it – life is different.

Something to Do

Are you ready for life to be different? If so, answer these questions.

- Do you love Jesus with all your heart, soul and mind? (We can only do this through the power of the Holy Spirit. If you are struggling with this, ask Him to help you.)

- What can you do to foster growth in your relationship with Jesus?

- How can you spend more time with Him?

- We know we can trust Him, but can He trust you?

Chapter 6
Doing My Part

We have established that we want to experience intimacy with Jesus. We want to take our relationship with Him to a place of mutual commitment. What does that look like?

In one of Dr. Robert Jeffress' daily devotionals[60] he shares the four levels of friendship:

- Acquaintances – People we have met, but do not share a relationship. Dr. Jeffress says in a year's time we make between 500 to 2500 acquaintances.

- Casual friends – Those we know on a first name basis, chat with occasionally, enjoy seeing, but keep our conversations superficial.

- Close friends – These are our tribe, inner circle, and running buddies. Dr. Jeffress says depending on our social network, our close friends can number from 5 to 25.

- Intimate friends – Those we share our deepest feelings with and feel safe being vulnerable and real. Regardless of how often we are together, the connection never waivers. Dr. Jeffress says we usually have no more than 6 intimate friends throughout our lifetime.

Looking at this list, would you say Jesus is an acquaintance of yours or a casual friend? Do you feel the two of you are close or have you grown to a place of intimacy? If we only develop six in a lifetime, it is safe to say we do not have a lot of experience growing intimate relationships.

To gain a little better understanding of what an intimate relationship looks like, let's look at what makes it special. Marla and I have been close since we were in the eighth grade. I cannot think of anything she does not know about me. No matter what I say or do, she knows my heart and who I am – therefore, she is not easily offended. Even when I am wrong, she never condemns me. Her love for me compels her to speak truth into my life and lovingly guide me to where I need to be, offering grace freely. She has been through every struggle with me, celebrates all my milestones in life and makes time to keep in close contact. She has never betrayed my trust and loves me unconditionally.

I know, she sounds a lot like Jesus, doesn't she? Well, that is my point. Marla is an incredible friend, but she is not perfect. Her friendship provides a glimpse of what Jesus offers us. He already loves us unconditionally – we do not have to earn it. He knows everything about us and knows our heart. He sees our value and our goodness. There is no condemnation,[61] in fact we are empowered to experience freedom because He is alive in us. Because of what Jesus has done for us, we have the Holy Spirit with us always, guiding us and helping us grow closer to Him. He loves us enough to guide us in truth, and offer His grace upon grace upon grace. Jesus is the best friend we will ever have.

Intimacy takes time to develop and requires two invested parties. Do you think Marla and I could be intimate friends if she was there for me and I was not equally committed? Of course not. The only way our relationship with Jesus can grow to this deep place is if we prove we aren't just enjoying His commitment to us, but we are showing up committed to Him.

Are we ready to be all in and committed to building this relationship? Are we ready to put Jesus *first* in our life, stop living for "me" and instead live for Him? Are we ready to act and get to know Him more than we do right now? It will never be easy or come naturally to put Jesus first. Matter of fact, you will have to fight for it.

You see, we have an adversary who will do anything to prevent us from developing intimacy with Jesus. He will do His best to distract you, throw obstacles in your way and whisper lies. As a child of God, you have nothing to fear when it comes to Satan. Our God is greater, stronger, and more powerful. We just need to be mindful of Satan's diversionary tactics and not fall prey to them.

Regardless of how many intimate friends we have here on earth, we can have One who exceeds them all. Where do we begin if we want to foster a growing relationship with Jesus?

Action Step 1: Study and Apply God's Word.

The Bible is God's word to us. It is our handbook for how to live the Christian life and offers answers to all the questions that swirl around in our head. *Why am I here? What is my purpose? Is there life after death? What should I do with my life? How should I parent my children? What does it mean to be a good spouse or a good friend? What matters in life? Where do I turn when I am suffering? How do I live the life I have been called to live? How do I put Jesus at the center of my life?*

We can read and gloss over God's word or we can study it and gain understanding. If I glance over an insurance form, I have no idea what it says. But if I break it down clause by clause and decipher it, I gain an understanding of it. The same is true of God's word.

It is only through understanding God's word that we can apply it in our daily life. That is the goal here: to study and apply God's word. We will get out of our time in God's word what we put into it. Think of it as mining for gold - search the surface and you will find some gold flakes, dig deeper and you will find nuggets; the deeper you dig the greater the reward.

Paul tells us,

All scripture is given by inspiration of God, and is profitable for doctrine, for reproof, for correction, for instruction in righteousness, that the man of God may be complete, thoroughly equipped for every good work.[62]

Well, if we take a few minutes and study these verses we will discover some nuggets.

Immediately, we see that every word in the Bible is inspired by God. The scripture says God's word is doctrine and doctrine is knowledge. Well, we need knowledge and information regarding how we should live. God offers us this instruction so we can live an abundant life built on the firm foundation of His word.

God's word is reproof and reproof leads to conviction. By reading God's word we will become aware of and burdened by the things we need to change in our life. It shines a light on our sin and on the areas that need growth.

This scripture tells us God's word is instruction. We know that instruction is teaching and is part of the process of raising or training a child. As our Heavenly Father, He is teaching us how to walk in obedience to Him. Apart from studying and understanding God's word, there is no other way to obey Him.

And lastly, this scripture says God's word is correction. We all wish we could go back to correct and undo mistakes, right, as though they were never there? Actually, we have something better - God's grace. He wipes the slate clean, covers our shame, binds our brokenness, and He restores us. Correction here refers to setting something straight. It involves making a change, getting things right, turning from our old ways and walking in His way. This correction prompts us to correct our thoughts, behaviors and actions that are not pleasing to our Lord.

In verse 17 we see that studying God's word will make us complete. Complete means whole, finished, perfected. Jesus is our soul mate - the only One who can complete us and satisfy us. He is all we need. We came to Jesus broken, ashamed and with a life in shambles and He not only accepted us, but forgave us and loves us unconditionally. He promised if we submit to Him, He will begin to work in us to perfect us and bring us to completeness. We will never be perfect, but we have an opportunity to grow, get to know Him and His ways, and be transformed. Just these two verses prove that jumping in and studying God's word is worth it! These two verses say a lot. Do you see the difference between reading and studying? Studying God's word will change your life. Ready?

Create a plan to make the time to study God's word. First thing in the morning is a great time because it prepares you for your day. If you are not a morning person, I feel your pain, but you might find it is worth it to get up a little bit earlier.

You see, we wake up and plan for what we think is going to happen that day, but God knows what lies ahead. By spending time with Him first, He will prepare us for the day He knows we are about to encounter. We will be prepared for the things we did not expect. I once heard a fitness expert say he recommended working out first thing in the morning, but it was better to work out at night than not at all. Making Bible study a part of your life is what matters most; you choose what time of day to make it happen.

Pick your time, get committed and do it. I really encourage you to invest in a good study Bible. Choose a translation you can understand yet remains faithful to the original text. A study Bible explains the verses, which is so helpful.

Visit www.pampegram.com for a free downloadable file with 10 Tips to Help You Study God's Word.

I am excited! You are going to fall in love with God's word! It is like drinking water - the more you drink, the more you crave. It may seem challenging at first, but you will begin to want more and more time in the Word. You will be amazed how God will use it in your life. It may take time for you to become comfortable with it and feel as if you comprehend anything at all, but hang in there and keep at it. Keep reading, keep studying and before you know it, it will come alive for you. You will feel as if God is speaking directly into your life and honestly, He will be. Feel free to put this book down and pick His up. But come back later because we are going to talk about more action steps.

Action Step #2: Spend time in prayer.

Prayer is simply talking to God. There is no need to try to sound spiritual or eloquent. God loves you just as you are, so be yourself when you talk with Him. After all, that is what friends do. They are free to be themselves when they are together. This is the only way to have a true relationship. Remember, God is sovereign and already knows everything about you, including your thoughts and feelings. There is no need to try to pretend or hide anything. You can be totally real with Him – even when it is not pretty.

As a Christian, we need to understand why we should pray and talk with God. First, we are commanded to pray throughout scripture, therefore it is an act of obedience. We are told to be *faithful in prayer*,[63] to *pray for those who persecute you*,[64] *by prayer...make your requests known to God*,[65] to *devote yourselves to prayer*,[66] and on and on. In 1 Thessalonians 5:17 we read, *"Pray without ceasing, in everything give thanks; for this is the will of God in Christ Jesus for you."* This does not mean to pray constantly; God knows we have conversations with others. It means to be persistent and consistent in prayer, making it an important part of our life.

We should pray because Jesus prayed. He came to be the living sacrifice for our sins and the perfect example of walking in obedience to God. Jesus got up early and prayed,[67] He prayed in the evening[68] and He spent the night praying to God.[69] He even gave us an example of how to pray.[70] Take time to read the Lord's prayer and take note that Jesus prayed to God, *"Your kingdom come. Your will be done."* The spirit in which we communicate is important. James warns us, *"You ask and do not receive, because you ask amiss, that you may spend it on your pleasures."*[71] You see, God is not our genie in a bottle waiting for us to make a wish. Instead of praying for our foolish desires, we should pray for God's will to be done.

After all, He knows what is best.

James even says that in our everyday speech, *"you ought to say, 'If the Lord wills, we shall live and do this or that'."*[72] We should submit our way and desire to live our life His way. That is a choice we will need to make each day. We can wake up and say, *I am not living life my way today. It is all about you, Jesus. Today, I am choosing to give up my way and submit to yours! Lead me, Lord! Guide me. Help me to walk in your will today.*

> *Today, I am choosing to give up my way and submit to yours! Lead me, Lord! Guide me. Help me to walk in your will today.*

Scripture teaches us Jesus prayed for others, prayed prayers of thanksgiving, prayed when He was troubled, called out to God in His time of need and prayed without ceasing, trusting God to hear His prayers. In Philippians 4:6-7 we read,

> *Be anxious for nothing, but in everything by prayer and supplication, with thanksgiving, let your requests be made known to God; and the peace of God, which surpasses all understanding, will guard your hearts and minds through Christ Jesus.*

Here God is telling us we should not worry or be anxious.

Instead take our concerns, needs, struggles and everything else to God in prayer. We can lay them at the foot of the cross, leave them there and trust God with the outcome. We can experience peace because we know He is in control.

This is the blessed life – not anxious to see far down the road nor overly concerned about the next step, not eager to choose the path nor weighted down with the heavy responsibilities of the future, but quietly following the Shepherd, one step at a time.[73]

Are you still concerned with *how* to pray? Prayer is how we communicate, and any relationship requires two-way communication. God speaks to us through His word. We speak to Him through prayer. When my children were little, I taught them they could talk to Jesus and He would hear them because He was always with them. If they were afraid they could pray, *Jesus, please be with me because I am scared.*

I had to chuckle one day when my three-year-old asked Jesus to help us because her baby sister's diaper *"sure did stink."* (Try keeping a straight face through that prayer.) She trusted Jesus to help us survive the aroma we were being subjected to in the car that day. Oh, we all need that child-like faith, don't we?

You too can talk to Jesus about anything. Whatever is on your mind, bothering you or whatever you are excited about, He is listening. He knows you, understands where you have been, all that has happened in your life, and the pain you have experienced. He gets it and will be faithful to use it – every tear, every heartache, every bad day - He will use for good in your life. Talk to Him; He is listening.

You cannot pray wrong. The goal is to get comfortable talking to God and then do it more and more often. Set aside time in your day to be still and talk to God. Also, make it a goal to keep growing until you find that you pray all throughout your day, applying the command to pray without ceasing. For example, when you wake, *Good morning, Lord. Thank you for this day and the opportunity to serve You.* As you walk out of your house, *Thank you God for this beautiful day and this sunshine.* As you read an email, *Lord, please show me how I should respond.* As you encounter a challenging situation, *Lord, help me to reflect You in this situation.*

If you are still uncomfortable and prefer a little structure, I can provide a guideline for how to pray. But please know, God hears every prayer, from the simplest to the most eloquent and I think He likes the simple ones best. Have you ever had someone start talking to you and you realized they were trying to impress you but it had the opposite effect? No need to try to impress God; He already deemed you worth dying for. When you start talking to Him, He is focused on hearing your heart.

If you want to follow a model to pray by until you feel more comfortable, visit www.pampegram.com and find a model of How to Pray. Spending time in prayer is investing in our relationship with Jesus. The more time we spend, the closer we will grow. That is our goal – *to grow an intimate relationship with Jesus.*

Action Step #3: Fellowship with Believers.

Someone reading this just sarcastically whispered, *Oh, great!* Actually, it is great. You see, we all need friends. Throughout the Bible we are encouraged to have relationships. Think about it for a minute. There are many, many scriptures telling us to love others. We are to love them and have relationships with them. Jesus had many relationships - with His family members, His followers, His disciples, and with God. Jesus came to earth as a man, lived a sinless life and died a sacrificial death. He came and walked where we walk, suffered how we suffer and lived as we are to live so we could relate to Him and have a relationship with Him.

I realize relationships come easier for some than others. Personalities, comfort zones and insecurities may come into play. But no matter, the scriptures teach us we are to build relationships because they are a big part of the Christian life. Practice growing in your people skills. Practicing the action steps we have talked about will help. As we spend more time in God's word and pray more, we will love a little deeper, offer forgiveness more freely and accept others for who they are.

You may be wondering if it is okay to build relationships with people who are not Christ followers. The answer is yes, *absolutely*. Develop relationships with others regardless of their beliefs. A relationship builds trust and trust gives you the opportunity to share Jesus with the lost and encourage believers who have lost their way. However, it is good to set healthy boundaries. You do not want to allow a relationship to influence you to sin or to distract you from growing in your relationship with Jesus. Guard yourself and remember it is easier for someone to pull you down than for you to lift them up. Love everyone but walk closely with Jesus.

Hebrews 10:24-25 says,

And let us consider one another in order to stir up love and good works, not forsaking the assembling of ourselves together, as is the manner of some, but exhorting one another and so much the more as you see the Day approaching.

What does this scripture tell us? First it says let us consider one another. Consider means "to observe" or "to contemplate" or "to have intelligent insight into."

Building a relationship with those who have a true and intimate relationship with Jesus will encourage us in our walk. We need mentors to lead us in our faith. It may be a pastor, a Sunday School teacher or small group leader, your mom or a sweet friend, or it may be a church member you have not even met yet. As you grow in your relationship with Christ, be willing to be the one encouraging new believers in their walk.

Okay, let's go back and read what that scripture says next. *"And let us consider one another in order to stir up love and good works."* Let's be honest here, who we hang out with determines what gets *stirred up* in our lives. Our friends can stir us up to do fun things that are fine, but they can also stir us up to do things we have no business doing. They can stir us up to sin, step onto the wrong path or to simply lose focus. We must remain diligent to follow Christ and not the crowd. As Christians, we are to love everyone, even our enemies. We are not to judge or think we are better than others. However, we are to be careful about who we allow to "stir us up." Make sense? So, we are to carefully choose our close relationships and purposefully add people to our lives who will encourage our Christian walk and stir us up to love others and do good works. Our sinful nature would rather gossip, resent others, and be self-centered, seeking to fulfill our personal desires for pleasure. So, we need friends who will encourage us to love as Christ loves, offer grace as He does and walk in humility as He did. Choose your relationships wisely.

There is more: *"Not forsaking the assembling of ourselves together."* We are to get together with other Christians. This assembling is referring to gathering together to worship God. In other words, we are to go to church. We will talk in detail about church later. But, just know the coming together of Christians to worship and praise our Creator is something we want as part of our life. It should be a very positive and powerful experience. It can be a part of your life that brings about blessings you never imagined.

The scripture ends saying we should be *"exhorting one another and so much the more as you see the Day approaching."* Exhorting means "to urge to do something," so by building relationships with fellow believers, we can come alongside one another to hold hands and travel this journey together. I like to think we are doing that in this book. We can relate to one another because we both desire to figure out how to live our life for Christ.

God's word is our step-by-step guide to who we should be, how we should live and what we are to do. When we assemble and study God's word, we learn how to apply it to our crazy, out-of-control, falling apart, struggle-filled, fear-induced lives. We have an opportunity to see others who have been where we are and have come through it victoriously by living out their faith, therefore being inspired to do the same. The church house is filled - not with perfect people, but with imperfect people all coming together because they desire to allow God to do a work in them, to perfect them, to grow them, to change them and to make them into who He is calling them to be.

These are our action steps to take our relationship with Christ to the next level:

- #1 – Study and apply God's word. It is the truth and will set us free!

- #2 – Spend time in prayer, building our relationship with Jesus. He is the best friend we will ever have.

- #3 – Make it a priority to fellowship with believers. We need to relate with one another to encourage and inspire each other in our relationship with Christ.

Putting it All Together

We have talked about who Jesus is and what He has done for us. We have learned the difference in practicing religion and building a relationship. We established that Jesus is committed to us - but, if we are to achieve our goal of intimacy with Jesus, we have to show our commitment to Him. We have some steps to take. It is time for us to prove our commitment by putting Him first, spending time studying His word, talking with Him in prayer and by fellowshipping with other believers because iron sharpens iron. It is time to do our part.

Today, why don't you take some time to have an authentic intimate conversation with Jesus?

Chapter 7

Becoming More Like Christ

Here we are, *Christians. What in the world does that mean?* Well, the definition in the dictionary says "a believer in Jesus Christ as Savior." That is correct, but falls short of what being a Christian is all about. The word Christian was first mentioned in the Bible in the book of Acts. After the persecution of Stephen - who was stoned for his belief – believers scattered to share the gospel and tell the good news. The Bible says, *"And the disciples were first called Christians in Antioch."*[74] Scholars believe they were called Christians because they were acting like Christ. The word may have been used to ridicule the believers, but they gladly accepted the title. If someone were to accuse us of acting like Christ, we should accept it as a compliment, don't you think?

> There is a big difference in acting Christ-like and becoming more like Christ.

As Christians, how do *we* act like Christ? Do we want to just *act* like Christ or is our goal to *become* like Christ? There is a big difference. Did you catch that? There is a big difference in *acting* Christ-like and *becoming* more like Christ.

Becoming like Jesus is a continual process that will only come to completion once we have entered the gates of Heaven. We cannot expect the transformation to be magical or happen overnight. We cannot expect it to be easy and without interference from our enemy. It requires surrender. It is a commitment and will come from spending time with Him and building a relationship with Him.

The Bible teaches that Jesus is the living word and the Bible is the written word. This is why it is so important to build a relationship with Jesus and to study the Bible. The more we do, the more knowledge and understanding we will gain and the more obedient we will become.

It's time to stop making excuses and start making room for Jesus in our life. We make time for everything else that is important to us, don't we? Carve out time every day for Him and before you know it you will be hooked on Him. You see, when we fall in love with Jesus, we want to spend time with Him. When we spend time with Him, we get to know Him. As we come to know Him more, we want to become more like Him. We start becoming Christ-like.

Have you experienced this in other relationships? You say something and suddenly realize, *I sound just like my mother.* (Then you roll your eyes. You know you do!) When we spend a lot of time around someone we often begin to talk like them and even pick up some of their mannerisms. As Christians, we want to spend a lot of time in the Word and in prayer so we can begin to speak and act like Christ. Please note - I am not saying thou shalt begin to becomest weird and playest a role. No. Be yourself, just better. Submit yourself to the Lord so you can grow and change and become the best YOU you can be. Our surrender to Him opens us up to allow God to grow us into who He created us to be. We can begin to take on His characteristics and become more and more like Him. Let's talk about some of the characteristics of Christ.

Before we do that, let's chat. Someone reading this may be thinking, *"Whatever! How can I become like Christ? You don't know me or what I have done or what I have been through."* I may not know you, but I get it. We all feel that way for one reason or another. Some of us have lived a life of reckless rebellion, living far from the Lord and everyone around us knows it. Others of us have lived what looked like a good life, yet have struggled with bitterness, anger, discontentment, fear, anxiety, jealousy, and many other secret sins.

But, please hear me, *it doesn't matter*. It doesn't matter unless you make it matter. Don't make the mistake of making what you have done bigger than what Jesus has done for you. God has offered you grace and full-on

> *Don't make the mistake of making what you have done bigger than what Jesus has done for you.*

forgiveness. All you need to do is ask for and embrace that forgiveness and then forgive yourself. I heard someone say once, *God has unlocked the prison door but now you have to walk out of the cell.* It is not about who you have been – it is about who you are becoming. Someone needed that today. Let's keep going.

I agree the thought of becoming like Christ is intimidating, but this is possible for us. 2 Corinthians 5:17 tells us,

> *Therefore, if anyone is in Christ, he is a new creation; old things have passed away; behold, all things have become new.*

When we accepted Jesus, we asked Him to forgive our sins and He did. We were given a chance to start over. Please don't cling to your past and prevent change from taking place. On this journey, we are going to stumble and maybe even fall. Every Christian you know stumbles - stop expecting Christians to be perfect and start allowing Christ to perfect you.

Let me share Romans 12:1-2 with you. Verse 1 says,

> *I beseech you therefore, brethren, by the mercies of God, that you present your bodies a living sacrifice, holy, acceptable to God, which is your reasonable service.*

Paul, who wrote Romans, is saying we should present our body as a living sacrifice to God, meaning we should serve and obey Him. The word holy means we are to be set apart for God's use. Acceptable means pleasing to God. Reasonable suggests our service is the only rational reaction we should have to all the gifts God has given to us, namely our salvation.

Side note: Did you know Paul, who wrote most of the New Testament and did extraordinary things for the Kingdom of God, was a persecutor of Christians? It is believed that he stood and held the cloaks of the men who stoned Stephen. He dragged Christians out of their homes and threw them in prison for their beliefs. Then one day, he had an encounter with God and everything changed. He was set free from who he had been and was made new in Christ. If God can transform Paul and use him, then He can transform you and use your life for His glory.

Verse 2 is my favorite. It says,

And do not be conformed to this world, but be transformed by the renewing of your mind, that you may prove what is good and acceptable and the perfect will of God.

We are not to be conformed to this world – self-centered, insecure, needy, longing to fit in, and going along with the crowd. But we should be transformed – changed by our salvation experience, *longing* to be like Christ, *willing* to be different, secure in who He is and who we are in Him, fulfilled, set apart, and full of joy. Get it? If you are thinking it will take a miracle to transform you – well, God is still in the business of performing miracles, so get ready because He is ready to do something great in you!

Let's look at three characteristics of Christ: love, forgiveness and humility.

Love

Jesus *is* Love. There are different types of love, but the Greek word used to describe the way Jesus loves us is *agape*. His love for us is unconditional and not based on our circumstances or our actions; no good performance is required. We haven't earned it and we certainly don't deserve it. Yet, we are His child and He is crazy about us.

I Corinthians 13:4-8 gives us a description of what this agape love looks like. It says,

> *Love suffers long and is kind; love does not envy; love does not parade itself, is not puffed up; does not behave rudely, does not seek its own, is not provoked, thinks no evil; does not rejoice in iniquity, but rejoices in the truth; bears all things, believes all things, hopes all things, endures all things. Love never fails.*

My Bible[75] contains an in-depth explanation of this scripture and I want to share it with you:

> *This word, agape, describes a love that is based on the deliberate choice of the one who loves rather than the worthiness of the one who is loved. This kind of love*

goes against natural human inclination. It is a giving, selfless, expect nothing in return kind of love. Paul's description of love is short but full of power.

Love suffers for a long time. Our modern "throw away" society encourages us to get rid of people in our lives who are difficult to get along with, whether they are friends, family or acquaintances. Yet this attitude runs in complete contrast to the love described by Paul. True love puts up with people who would be easier to give up on.

Love does not envy. If our love is directed toward others, we will rejoice in the blessing they receive rather than desiring those blessings for ourselves. Fundamentally, the selfless love that God calls us to does not involve pride or glory. It does not parade itself and is not puffed up. In fact, true love does not seek its own. If we truly love others, we will set aside our own plans, agendas, and entitlements for the good of another.

Love is not provoked. That is, love is not easily angered or over-sensitive. When we truly love others, we are careful not to be touchy concerning other people's words or actions towards us.

Love does not rejoice in iniquity, but rejoices in the truth. The godly love described in this chapter has nothing to do with evil, but has everything to do with what is right and true. It believes all things and hopes all things. This does not mean that love is blind or naïve. When we love, we may recognize problems and failures in people, but we do not lose faith in the possibilities of what people might become. Love never gives up, knowing that God can change lives for the better.

Finally, love endures all things. Love accepts any hardship or rejection, and continues unabated to build up and encourage. The love described by Paul in this "love chapter" means determining what is best for another person and doing it. This is the kind of love that God shows to us.

This is who God is and how He loves. This is how we are to love others. Jesus says, *"By this all will know that you are My disciples, if you have love for one another."*[76] Can we do it? Well, not on our own. We need God's help to learn to love like He does. What a gift and a blessing to be able to offer unconditional love to others.

Let's pray and ask for that help right now. *"Jesus, please help us. We need an intervention. This type of love is not normal for us, but we no longer want to be normal. We want to be changed. We want to be different. We want You to transform us. We want to become more like You and love with Your kind of love. Please help us, Lord. Please help us see beyond our thoughts, our desires and our feelings. Help us see people the way You see them and love them – unconditionally – just like You do. In Your name we pray. Amen!"*

Forgiveness

Another characteristic of Jesus is forgiveness. If you have ever watched a depiction of the crucifixion of Christ, then you know it was horrendous. The pain and humiliation Jesus endured for us was unimaginable. But at the end of His life - after being falsely accused, beaten unmercifully, humiliated, mocked, and nailed to a cross – He prayed for His aggressors saying, *"Father forgive them, for they do not know what they do."*[77] Can you imagine? Doesn't that just blow you away? After all He endured and all they had done to Him, He offered them forgiveness and grace. Grace is forgiveness that is not deserved.

We as Christ followers are called to offer this same type of forgiveness to others. We all have people in our lives we can proclaim do not deserve our forgiveness. We may be right, but our example – Jesus – showed us how to forgive those who do not deserve to be forgiven. He has forgiven each of us and we have not earned it and do not deserve it.

You see, like love, forgiveness is a choice. Forgiveness is not a fruit of the spirit. Fruits of the spirit are intended to grow in us as we grow in our relationship with our Savior. But forgiveness is an action, an act of our will. If we desire to be like Christ, it is a choice we must make over and over throughout our lives. I realize that is not exciting and in all honesty, is very hard, but stay with me.

Why must we forgive those who have wronged us? Well, because Jesus says,

> *For if you forgive men their trespasses, your heavenly Father will also forgive you. But if you do not forgive men their trespasses, neither will your Father forgive your trespasses.*[78]

In Mark 11:25, it says,

> *And whenever you stand praying, if you have anything against anyone, forgive him, that your Father in heaven may also forgive you your trespasses.*

There are many more scriptures about forgiveness. God makes it very clear; *we are to forgive.* I have searched and searched and there is no "*if*" after that command. So, that means no matter what, we are to forgive.

In some situations, forgiveness seems impossible. Others who love us and think they are protecting us may even encourage our hatred or resentment to grow, helping us to justify it and giving us permission to stay stuck in our bitterness. But remember, God sent us a helper. He is there to help us release it and replace it with grace. He will carry our pain and bear our burden. We can ask Him to help us to forgive.

Although we forgive, we are not required to forget. "Forgive and forget" is not in the Bible. Some things are petty and should be forgotten, but sometimes not forgetting offers us the opportunity to learn from our experiences.

When Jesus asked God to forgive those who had beaten Him, He had not forgotten what He had endured. However, remembering does not mean harboring resentment. Instead of dwelling on the transgression, we can lay it down and allow God to use it to grow and change us.

I need to clarify that forgiveness does not mean we place ourselves in dangerous situations or stay in unhealthy relationships. Sometimes, healthy boundaries must be established to keep us physically or emotionally safe. We can still forgive and separate ourselves from those situations. The Holy Spirit should be your guide here. Ask Him to show you what to do, read God's word and listen intently to those promptings.

Then, there are everyday things that make us mad and angry – traffic, people who disappoint us and family members who annoy us. Many of these things we can just let go. We can learn to be great grace-givers. People are struggling and hurting. People are lost and don't have the hope our relationship with Jesus offers. Ephesians 4:31-32 tells us,

Let all bitterness, wrath, anger, clamor, and evil speaking be put away from you, with all malice. And be kind to one another, tenderhearted, forgiving one another, even as God in Christ forgave you.

Let's all make a commitment to challenge ourselves to offer grace. God has rained down His grace on us, therefore, we can share a little grace in our everyday life. We can stop placing expectations on others and harboring resentment when they do not live up to them. We are not God. He is and they need to please Him, not us. For those who have wronged us in a big way, God will help us to forgive. We can lay it down at the foot of the cross. We can give it to God and let Him deal with it. He is our defender. We no longer need to allow our lack of forgiveness to hold us prisoner to our pain. We can break free today!

Humility

Jesus is humble. Take a minute and think about who Jesus is and what He has done. He is our Savior, the King of Kings, the Lord of Lords, the Lamb of God, the Great I Am and so on and so forth. Yet, He left His throne to come to earth and live as a mere man. If that was not enough, as an adult He left His earthly home and family and became homeless. He walked among men and He served people. He humbled Himself all the way to the point of death. What a perfect picture of humility, selflessness, and complete love. Jesus is our model for humility. Matthew 20:28 says, *"just as the Son of Man did not come to be served, but to serve, and to give His life a ransom for many."* If we are to be Christ-like or like Christ in any way, we must be humble, willing to serve others and present our life to Him as a sacrifice. We should proclaim, *Not my way, Lord – but yours.*

The world or our society tells us those who are deemed great by earthly standards should be honored and pampered and have a house full of servants. Jesus says in Matthew 23:11-12, *"But he who is greatest among you shall be your servant. And whoever exalts himself will be humbled, and he who humbles himself will be exalted."* Now that is a different approach to life, isn't it? It is refreshing when we encounter humble people and even more so when they are in a place of leadership.

So, what does this scripture mean? Does it mean we are to quit our day jobs and seek employment as a household servant? No. Jesus is talking about servanthood. You see, it does not matter how high our position is in the workplace, church, or family, we are all called to serve. It is about our attitude and our heart. Jesus was the King of Kings and the Lord of Lords, yet He was a Servant Leader. He served others as He led them to the cross and into the hope of salvation.

So, how do we become humble and pleasing to the Lord? To be humble by biblical terms is to be meek in spirit and selfless. This does not mean we should think less of ourselves – after all we are a child of the King. No, it means we are to think of ourselves less often. Philippians 2:3 tells us,

Let nothing be done through selfish ambition or conceit, but in lowliness of mind let each esteem others better than himself.

We can be so full of ourselves – focusing on our wants, needs, disappointments, insecurities and desires. We are filled with pride and seek approval and praise. But, none of those things are Christ-like, are they?

Learning to be humble is about falling in love with Jesus and coming to the realization that every good and perfect gift comes from Him – every breath, every step, every accomplishment, every moment of laughter, every bit of knowledge, and every relationship we have is all because of Him and how good He is.

Let's chat about a few practical ways we can humble ourselves. We drive as if where we are going is most important and everyone needs to get out of our way. We park our car as if we should not have to take extra steps into the store. We want the best seats, the best view, the biggest office, the smartest phone, to tell the best story, and to have the most friends. We can humble ourselves by allowing someone to get over in front of us in traffic, motion for someone to take the parking place, listen to someone's story without trumping it with ours, and we can arrive on time instead of expecting others to wait on us. We can come to the realization that neither our day or even our life is about us. Everything - and I do mean everything - is all about God We are put here to serve Him and to lead others to Him. Now apply that example to every area of our life.

We can begin every day by choosing to humble ourselves before the One who gave His life for us. We can choose to be like Him and put others before our own wants and needs. I love Philippians 2:5-11,

Let this mind be in you which was also in Christ Jesus, who being in the form of God, did not consider it robbery to be equal with God, but made Himself of

no reputation, taking the form of a bondservant, and coming in the likeness of men. And being found in appearance as a man, He humbled Himself and became obedient to the point of death, even the death of the cross. Therefore, God also has highly exalted Him and given Him the name which is above every name, that at the name of Jesus every knee should bow, of those in heaven, and of those on earth and of those under the earth, and that every tongue should confess that Jesus Christ is Lord, to the glory of God the Father.

That is who we are called to become like. Overwhelming? It is! But, here is the deal. When we choose to become like Him, we are set free! For the first time in our lives we are *free* from guilt and shame, *free* from the need to gain approval of others, *free* to become who we have been created to be, and *free* to become alive in Him. We stop striving and start surrendering our life to Christ who surrendered His life for us. Then and only then can we experience joy no matter our circumstances.

> *We stop striving and start surrendering our life to Christ who surrendered His life for us.*

To become like Christ, we must surrender our ALL. We must surrender our pride, our position, our feelings, our attitude, our strongholds, and even our insecurities. Those are all part of our sinful nature and they are to be crucified with Christ.[79] We are to present our bodies as a living sacrifice to God. Just as Jesus was sacrificed for us, we are to sacrifice our worldly selves for Him.

Let's be honest. It is easy to not love others, easy to not offer forgiveness and easy to be anything other than humble. Becoming like Christ is guaranteed to be hard. But we are not called to do easy, we are called to do hard. It is hard to love everyone unconditionally, offer grace freely and walk in humility. Just like we have been crucified with Christ, we have also been resurrected with Him. The transforming power alive in us makes this possible.

Without Him, we would surely fail, but because of Him we can love, forgive and humble ourselves in a way that will draw others to Jesus. We are not trying to become someone others will admire. We are becoming Christ-like so others will see Him alive in us and want to have Him alive in them as well. Because He chose to die for us, we can choose to live for Him. Philippians 1:6 says,

Being confident in this very thing, that He who has begun a good work in you will complete it until the day of Jesus Christ.

Something to Ponder

My way wants me to conform to this
world, to fit in, to be liked.

God's way wants me to be different,
to stand out, to be like Him.

Chapter 8
What Does He Want from Me?

We have a gift for making things complicated, don't we? We make intimacy with Jesus more difficult than it needs to be. So, if you are feeling a bit overwhelmed or simply not sure what it is God wants from you, let's just cut to the chase - *"Submit to God. Resist the devil and he will flee from you. Draw near to God and He will draw near to you."*[80] We need to submit.

I am not sure why we struggle with the word "submit." The definition is simple: to accept or yield to authority. Surely, by now we all realize God has *all authority* and is the Ruler of *All*. However, He is not a tyrant who wishes to hold us captive. We can freely submit our life, our thoughts, our actions, and *our all* to Him because He is the good and loving Father who knows what is best for each of us. He sets boundaries to protect us and He uses all things for good in our lives.

When we submit our life to God, we are resisting the devil. If we are not resisting Satan, then we are not submitting to Christ. It is that simple. If we resist and submit, then Satan will flee. But my favorite part is that if we draw near to God, then He will draw near to us. He asks us to submit our life to Him. He has given us all we need. Now, it's time for us to submit to Him by choosing to worship Him, obey Him and make room for Him.

Worship

Worship is defined as a feeling or expression of reverence and adoration for a deity (God). Jesus said "*for it is written, 'You shall worship the Lord your God, and Him only you shall serve.'*"[81] Worship begins with the acknowledgment of who God is. He is the Creator, the Ruler, the Father of all. He is the Supreme Being, perfect in power, goodness and wisdom. He is infinite, unchanging, the GREAT I AM! He is sovereign, holy and just. He is love and grace. He is the One – the only One we can truly believe in and trust, who will never leave us or disappoint us. He is the only One who will ever satisfy us. Worship begins with acknowledging our Almighty God.

Do you know that within each of us, God has placed a yearning, a great desire to worship Him and to seek Him? But sometimes we get that yearning confused and we put idols in His place because we are groping for something and live in denial that it is Him we need. We foolishly create little 'g' gods and in our ignorance put them in place of our Almighty God and worship them. I know I have done this and my guess is you have as well. Will you take a few minutes and ask God to reveal who or what it is that sits on the throne of your heart? (*Show me, Lord! Open my eyes and my heart and reveal anything I put before You.*)

Do you worship your man, believing he is your soulmate and living your life to please him? I have done that. I made a man my savior and gave him more importance in my life than God. It ended badly, with great pain and destruction left in its path. I now know Jesus is my soulmate and He is the One who truly satisfies and meets my needs. We are to love and respect our mate, but when we cross the line and worship them, we are choosing to believe they validate us and make our lives worth living. That is dangerous. We must be careful to not make our spouse *our Jesus*, expecting them to fulfill our needs. Only Jesus can do that. When we let Jesus be Jesus and our spouse be our partner, our friend and our cherished gift, the expectations fall away and peace and joy come to reside in our marriage.

Sometimes as parents, we allow ourselves to worship our children. We place them on a pedestal and if we are not careful, our lives begin to revolve around them. We become focused on living for and living to please our children. It was never meant to be this way. The love for a child is so great we can become confused and it can evolve into worship.

I remember rocking one of my sweet babies and having an honest conversation with God. *Really, God? How in the world am I supposed to love You more than I love this child?* In that moment, it was as if God whispered, *if you don't love Me most, you will never be able to love this child the way she deserves to be loved and be the mom she deserves to have.* Well, there you go. We should never do our children the disservice of making them our god. It will cripple them and leave scars we never intended to cause. Instead, we can realize that our love for our children is only a glimpse of how much God loves us. What we are willing to do for our babies pales in comparison to what Jesus has done for us. Therefore, let's walk out before them what it looks like to love the Lord our God with all our heart, soul and mind.

Maybe you worship your idol, your body image, your career, your success, your riches or something that brings you great pleasure. Make a list of the things you put before God. Be honest about what consumes you, what you worship. Here is what I know for sure –our career, money, fame, riches, bodies, sex, alcohol and drugs are all sure to disappoint. None of those are what life is all about. Life is not about *me* and what makes *me* happy.

> *Pursue Him with all your heart, fall madly in love with Him and you will come to understand true worship.*

Life is all about God. He created the world we live in and the very air we breathe. He has created us and given us a purpose. Our purpose is *not* to be blissfully happy, rich, the life of the party or to live in the biggest house on the street. Our purpose is to worship our King, live a life of obedience to Him and surrender to His will so He can use us to further His kingdom. Listen, I know it is crazy and hard to understand, but pursue Him with all your heart, fall madly in love with Him and you will come to understand true worship. He will satisfy you and you will find you have all you need. (I hope this is rocking your world! Read this paragraph again, it wrecks me each time I do.)

As God spoke the Ten Commandments to Moses He said, *"You shall have no other gods before Me."*[82] That is a pretty clear statement. God goes on to tell us,

> *For I, the Lord your God, am a jealous God, visiting the iniquity of the fathers upon the children to the third and fourth generations of those who hate Me, but showing mercy to thousands, to those who love Me and keep My commandments.*[83]

God is good and is simply making sure we understand that when we worship anything other than Him, our descendants will suffer. Jennifer Rothschild says that what we dabble in, our children will embrace. That is scary. Dabble in believing other things are more important than God and your children and their children will embrace that as truth. There are always consequences for our actions and our choices, but when we love God and worship Him and Him alone, the lingering effects of righteousness will be great.

I believe if we acknowledge who God is and put Him first in our life, worship will come naturally. God knows our heart and He knows when our worship is genuine, when it is stifled and when we are doing it for show. As our hearts are purified and we grow in our relationship with Jesus, we will want to worship Him by singing praises to His Holy name, walking in obedience to Him and surrendering everything to Him.

Obey

Submitting our life to God requires walking in obedience to Him. When we choose to obey God's word it sets us *free*! Many times, believers debate what they think they should or should not do. Can I be honest and tell you our opinion does not matter? What *does* matter is the instruction God has given to each of us in His word, the example Jesus lived out for us to follow and the promptings of the Holy Spirit.

We read in 1 John 5:3, *"For this is the love of God, that we keep His commandments. And His commandments are not burdensome."* You see the love of God demands our obedience, but we are not to be burdened and held captive by a strict list of rules. Our obedience sets us free to be who we were created to be and reflect the image of God. Because we love God, it is our pleasure to obey Him.

Remember when Adam and Eve chose to disobey and eat the apple; they were deceived and their eyes were opened? Their sin caused them to feel ashamed, so they hid. God called to them and Adam told Him he was afraid because he was naked. In Genesis 3:11 God says, *"Who told you that?"* What a profound question. It is a question we need to ask ourselves often. Who told you that? Are our beliefs based on our opinions, what our parents told us, what our friends believe, Satan's deceit or on God's truth? We need to know God's word and walk in obedience to it.

In John, Jesus tells us,

As the Father loved Me, I also have loved you, abide in My love. If you keep My commandments, you will abide in My love, just as I have kept My Father's commandments and abide in His love.[84]

The love Jesus has for us is unconditional. It is already ours, so we can stop trying to earn it by following rules. However, as we obey His word, we will come to understand and experience His love more and more.

These things I have spoken to you, that My joy may remain in you, and that your joy may be full. This is my commandment, that you love one another as I have loved you.[85]

Jesus is talking with His disciples and telling them all they need to know to experience the abundant life He came to offer us. He says we are to love others the way He loves us. Our obedience to His commands yields peace and joy in our life. He goes on to say,

Greater love has no one than this, than to lay down one's life for his friends. You are My friends if you

do whatever I command you. No longer do I call you servants, for a servant does not know what his master is doing; but I have called you friends, for all things have I heard from My Father I have made known to you. You did not choose Me, but I chose you and appointed you that you should go and bear fruit, and that your fruit should remain, that whatever you ask the Father in My name, He may give you. These things I command you, that you love one another.[86]

As Jesus was preparing to die for us, He asked that we live for Him by laying down our self-centeredness and walking in obedience to the Father the way He, the Son, had done.

Where do we begin with our obedience? You just want a list, right? Sorry, but that is not how this works. Remember, we are not looking to just methodically follow the rules. No ma'am! We want more than that; we want intimacy! Intimacy begins with acknowledgment. Just like we do not keep it a secret when we get married or have a baby, we should not keep this relationship a secret. We read in Romans 10:9-10, we are to confess with our mouth and acknowledge who Jesus is. We are not to be ashamed and keep our acceptance into this Holy family confidential. We are to boldly proclaim we have accepted Jesus as our Savior and will now live for Him.

One way to do that is to be baptized. In Romans 6:4 we learn,

Therefore we were buried with Him through baptism into death, that just as Christ was raised from the

*dead by the glory of the Father, even so we also should
walk in newness of life.*

Paul explains that baptism is an illustration of us being
identified with Christ. Jesus' death and the death of our old
ways is symbolized by our being submerged in the water.
And just as Jesus was raised from the dead, our coming
out of the water illustrates our newness of life in Him. In
Matthew 3:13-17, we read that Jesus was baptized, therefore
we should be, too. It is our announcement to the world that
we are a born-again Christian.

By accepting Jesus as our Savior, we have become
adopted into the family of God. The family of God is called
the body of Christ and sometimes simply called *the church*.
The church is not a building; it encompasses all believers.
Therefore, our Father wants us to come together with our
family to love one another, encourage one another and to
worship together.[87]

Don't make excuses or justify not being a part of the
church. When we join a gym, we do not walk out if every
person in the gym is not fit. We do not quit going if there
is an instructor teaching a class we do not enjoy. We quit
because we are not committed to being fit. Now, apply that
to attending church. We should not get upset if we see
sinners in the church. After all, you and I will be there, so
we are certain to find other imperfect people. We should be
inviting lost people to join us. Maybe God can use you to
inspire others to have a relationship with Jesus.

We are not putting our faith in the people or the pastor,
we are putting our faith in the Prince of Peace! Scripture

teaches us there is benefit to fellowshipping with believers and learning from those who are more mature in their faith. You can choose where you go to church and who mentors you; just remember, quitting church all together says a lot about your commitment to obedience and ultimately your intimacy with Christ.

We need to make sure the group of believers we do church with has a set of beliefs that line up with what the Bible teaches. We want to attend a church that is spiritually healthy for us. Pray and ask the Holy Spirit to give you wisdom and discernment as you look for a Bible-preaching, Bible-teaching church. Make sure they believe and teach the following: that the Bible is the infallible word of God; it is relevant today; that Jesus is the Way, the Truth and the Life and no one comes to the Father except through Him; and that the Holy Spirit is our helper and dwells within those who have accepted Jesus as their Savior.

Once you find a church that believes and teaches the Bible's truth and you feel a prompting this is where you belong, get plugged in and be an active member. Sing; God says so (smiley face). Singing praises to the Lord can be a power-filled time of worship. Psalms 98:1 says, *"Oh sing to the Lord a new song, for He has done marvelous things."* Verse 4 says, *"Make a joyful noise to the Lord, all the earth; break forth into joyous song and sing praises!"* Go to church ready to praise and worship the One who has poured out His amazing grace on you.

Become active by finding a place to serve. Take your Bible and take notes. Listen, learn, study and grow. Join a small group Bible study. Go to church to offer up your worship and praise to the Lord and to fellowship with believers. Sunday just might become your favorite day of the week.

We can be obedient by bringing our tithe to God. Do you know nothing belongs to us? Everything we have, we have by the grace of God. Everything we have belongs to Him, yet He allows us to be stewards of our blessings. He only asks that we bring our tithe to Him. We are not giving Him anything; it already belongs to Him. However, we can bring it back to Him. Bringing Him our tithe is part of worshiping Him and demonstrating our trust in Him. The Bible says to give our first fruits, which means to tithe first instead of waiting to see what is left over. Tithing demonstrates our obedience and trust in the Lord. Let's keep our hearts pure and tithe because we love God and desire to please Him.

In addition to our tithe, we as Christians should develop a giving spirit.

But this I say: He who sows sparingly will also reap sparingly, and he who sows bountifully will also reap bountifully. So let each one give as he purposes in his heart, not grudgingly or of necessity; for God loves a cheerful giver. And God is able to make all grace abound toward you, that you, always having all sufficiency in all things, may have an abundance for every good work.[88]

A giving spirit might include adding a little extra to our tithe, donating to charities, giving a coat to a needy child, feeding the homeless, saving the last cookie for your spouse, letting someone go in front of you, giving of your time to help someone and so many other things. Remember, we are to be transformed and no longer like the rest of the world – greedy and self-centered. Allow God to develop a giving spirit within you. Try it - I am pretty sure you will like it.

Those are a few ways we can begin this quest for obedience. But remember, obedience happens when we heed Jesus' command in Matthew 6:33 to *"Seek ye first the kingdom of God and His righteousness..."* He is the answer and He wants our complete obedience. Obedience simply means whispering a one-word prayer, yes. *Whatever you ask of me, Lord, yes.*

More of Him, Less of Me

I wish I was sitting face-to-face with you with a big mug of coffee - with a generous spot of cream, of course. I would set my cup down and tell you that God does not want us to be closed off from Him with our arms folded across our chest. That is not submission, that is a prideful, fear-filled stance that stifles our faith. Instead, we are to uncross our arms, open our hearts, and raise our hands high to the Heavens in total surrender to our King. Will you just lay this book down and try that? Raise your hands high and whisper, *more of You, Lord, less of me. Fill my heart with You, Jesus. I want more of You.* (Repeat it over and over, if necessary.)

If our heart was a pie chart, what would it look like?

How much would be shaded by our needs, desires and feelings? How big would Jesus' piece of our heart pie be? That hurts, doesn't it? He is worthy of so much more. So how do we make room for God in our life? How do we experience more of Him? We spend time with Him – praying, studying, worshipping, and walking with Him. We exchange what we want for what He has for us. We surrender every area of our life and live in submission to Him.

A.W. Tozer said it this way:

O God, be Thou exalted over my possessions. Nothing of earth's treasures shall seem dear unto me if only Thou art glorified in my life. Be Thou exalted over my friendships. I am determined that Thou shalt be above all, though I must stand deserted and alone in the midst of the earth. Be Thou exalted above my comforts. Though it mean the loss of bodily comforts and the carrying of heavy crosses I shall keep my vow made this day before Thee. Be Thou exalted over my reputation. Make me ambitious to please Thee even if as a result I must sink into obscurity and my name be forgotten as a dream. Rise, O Lord, into Thy proper place of honor, above my ambitions, above my likes and dislikes, above my family, my health and even my life itself. Let me decrease that Thou mayest increase, let me sink that Thou mayest rise above. Ride forth upon me as Thou didst ride into Jerusalem mounted upon the humble little beast, a colt, the foal of an ass, and let me hear the children cry to Thee, "Hosanna in the highest."[89]

Submitting our life to Christ requires worship, obedience and transformation. We give Him all He asks of us and we receive *all* His promises. Every. Single. One. All of God's promises are for us. Today is a great day to read Philippians 3:7-14. Be sure to grab your Bible and read Paul's words. Paul tells us he has learned that everything he thought was important is not. The value of knowing Christ surpasses everything else.

Something to Do

There is something to be said about writing scripture. Studies show that words written are more likely to be comprehended and remembered. So, take a few minutes to look up and write out Philippians 3:7-14.

_____

_____

_____

_____

_____

_____

_____

_____

_____

_____

_____

_____

_____

_____

_____

_____

Chapter 9

Living My Faith

As the alarm clock sounded, I gasped as the realization hit me all over again. *Oh God, is this really happening? Is this real or a bad dream? How did I get here?* I sat up and immediately felt a tear trail down my face. My head hurt and I felt too weak to go about my day.

It didn't matter how I was feeling; I had responsibilities. The kids needed to get up and get ready for school. They needed a mom who was present and ready to help them go through their day. Yet, here I sat dazed and confused, still finding it hard to believe. My happily ever after had imploded once again. Divorce #2, how could that be? I had been happy for fourteen years and never saw this coming. How would I survive?

My devotional lay on the nightstand. *Not today,* I thought. I was too exhausted to care what God had to say. I stared at it, mumbling under my breath, *I know! I need You, Lord, more than ever.* So I reached for it, begrudgingly flipped it open and began to read about someone who was overwhelmed by the affliction in their life. "I can relate," I sarcastically whispered. I went on to read about how she stood before an overgrown garden full of weeds and grass and heard God whisper into her spirit. She was reminded that the gardener stops pruning the vines, pulling the weeds and mowing the grass when He no longer expects anything from the garden during that season. He will leave it alone because its fruit bearing has come to an end. The scripture on the page was John 15:2,

> *Every branch in Me that does not bear fruit He takes away. Every branch that bears fruit, He prunes, that it may bear more fruit.*[90]

The story illustrated how our struggles and trials are used to prune us, grow us or prepare us, so we can bear fruit for Him. The next sentence leapt off the page at me. "Shall I leave you alone?" *What? What did that say?* "Shall I leave you alone?" What a profound question. *No, that is not what I want, I thought.* The realization hit me. While we are never eager to invite hard times into our lives, we certainly dare not ask God to just leave us alone, right? If we never experience anything hard, how can we grow or become stronger or even learn to trust in God? How would we ever come to know how good He is?

As Christians, we are called to live a life of faith. *"Faith is the substance of things hoped for, the evidence of things not seen."*[91] Faith is more than mere belief. The Bible tells us that demons know God is real and believe in Him. So, then what is faith? Faith is *trust* in God, dependence on God and is exemplified in our decision to rely on God. Do you have faith? Trusting, depending and relying on God is where we need to be headed. We need to live a life totally dependent on our faith in Jesus Christ. He needs

> *Faith is trust in God, dependence on God and is exemplified in our decision to rely on God.*

to be what guides and directs our steps. He needs to be what drives our purpose. He needs to be what sustains us.

It is time we stop relying on ourselves and doing things our way. Instead, we are to transition to the place where we rely on God and do life His way. Who besides me is mumbling "is that even possible?" Well, it is possible, because God says it is. Proverbs 3:5-6 tells us,

Trust in the Lord with all your heart, and lean not on your own understanding. In all your ways acknowledge Him and He shall direct your paths.

What does *"In all your ways acknowledge Him"* mean? Studying this scripture, I found that acknowledge means to observe the Lord, to get to know Him and study His word. Romans 10:17 says, *"So then faith comes by hearing, and hearing by the word of God."* By immersing ourselves in the Word of God, we come to the realization that without Him we are fools and do not make good choices. Apart from Him, we are sure to mess things up. We are hopeless without Him.

Walking out our faith is easy on beautiful, sunny days where everything is going our way. But what about the dark days, the days we experience hardships and difficulties, the days our faith is tested? Are we filled with faith on those days or is it fear that fills us? Time to be honest - we fail at faith, don't we? Worry, fear, and insecurity are all opposites of faith. What do you believe? In what have you placed your faith? Many times, we put our trust in our own abilities, instead of in the One we call our Savior. If we believe He has saved us from the depths of hell, then surely we can muster up enough faith to believe He can get us through our worldly struggles, losses and hardships. Here are some truths we can cling to no matter what might come our way.

Jesus is Enough

Living out our faith begins when we realize that Jesus is enough, He truly is all we need. We buy into Satan's lies when we choose to believe we need *to get this job, to have a husband, to start a family, to live in that neighborhood, to attain that title,* etc. There is nothing wrong with wanting a good job or a nice home, but none of those things matter to the extent that we make them matter. There is a difference in what we want and what we need. *We need Jesus.* Every day, He is enough.

It was in the most difficult time of my life when I learned this truth. I was in the process of accumulating what I thought I needed - a man, children, success, financial security - and feeling good about it when it all came tumbling down. I am being real with you, praying that baring my shortcomings will inspire you to get this. We believe Jesus is enough to save us, but we struggle to believe He is enough to sustain us. Oh, my friend, He is all you need.

What about our dreams and our goals? Psalm 37:4 says, *"Delight yourself in the Lord, and He shall give you the desires of your heart."* Now, let's use our sound mind to process that. Do we believe that if I am delightful and happy in the Lord, He will grant my desire to be a millionaire? Do we think our worldly desires matter? Or does that scripture mean that when we come to love God so much we find *delight in Him* then our desires will also spring forth from Him? And when our desires come from Him, He will surely fulfill them. Walking out our faith includes trusting God to help us define our desires. We want His desire for us to become our desires in Him. When those two things line up, we will find ourselves living a life that is exceedingly, abundantly above all we could have ever dared to imagine.[92]

> *Walking out our faith includes trusting God to help us define our desires.*

Not only is He enough to sustain us, but He offers all the affirmation we need. We do not need to please all the people in our life; as a matter of fact, we never will. Why is it we can have 1,000 people tell us they like us and think we are great, then one rolls her eyes at us and we fall to pieces? Our identity, our worthiness and our good-enoughness (Yes, I made that word up.) comes from Him and Him alone. The scriptures tell us He delights in us, is with us, has saved us, rejoices over us with gladness and with singing, quiets us with His love, and will never leave us. In Him, we are enough! Because of Him, we are worthy.

Jesus is enough to carry us through whatever this fallen world might throw at us. He is our strength, our fortress, and our rock. Even when we struggle to walk out our faith, He remains faithful to us. He will fulfill His promises to us. I can testify that He has proven *"I can do all things through Christ who strengthens me"*[93]; *"all things [even heartbreak] work together for good to those who love God, to those who are the called according to His purpose"* [94]; and He will *"supply all your needs according to His riches in glory by Christ Jesus."*[95] Today, trust that He is enough.

Jesus First and Foremost

Living out our faith means putting Jesus first in our lives. All good Christian girls will tell you they put Jesus first, their family second and then their career. It is one thing to say it, but altogether different to live it. It is only when we put Jesus first that we can become who we are meant to be, fulfill the purpose He has for us, become the wife our husband deserves, the mom our children need, and the friend so many women crave.

How do we do it?

- We put Him first by seeking Him as soon as our eyes open in the morning; reading our Bible and spending time in prayer with Him. He should get our first communication.

- We can seek Him first by allowing Him to direct our path, instead of us asking Him to bless the path we have chosen to walk.

- We can seek Him first by understanding that everything we have is a gift from him – our breath, our children, our job, our belongings. They are His and have been entrusted to us. We should be thankful instead of foolishly believing we have earned them on our own.

- We can seek Him first by tithing and bringing Him our "first fruits," and by trusting Him to meet our needs.

The guidance and direction Jesus provides is much more trustworthy than our feelings. Can I get an AMEN? John 3:30 says, *"He must increase, but I must decrease."* We should be more like Him, less like me. People hurt us and our feelings tell us to be angry and resentful, but Jesus showed us by example to offer grace. He did not yell and demand an apology. He chose to love and offer forgiveness. What about when our feelings tell us not to serve, not to give or to quit and give up? What if our feelings tell us we

have things under control and are doing great all by ourselves? What if they tell us we have no value or to enter a
relationship that is not healthy? What if our feelings pull
us toward doing things that are not pleasing to the Lord?
Are we to listen to our feelings? We, as women, often begin
our sentences with "I feel like..." Be warned, feelings are not
trustworthy.

Jesus is trustworthy. He is the Living Word and God's
word is trustworthy. We read in Colossians 3:1-4,

> *If then you were raised with Christ, seek those things
> which are above, where Christ is, sitting at the right
> hand of God. Set your mind on things above, not on
> things on the earth. For you died, and your life is
> hidden with Christ in God. When Christ who is our
> life appears, then you also will appear with Him
> in glory.*

Walking out our faith means choosing to seek those things
which are from God - His will, His way, a relationship with
Jesus. Putting Jesus first keeps our feelings out of the way.

Choose the Right Path

Walking out our faith is a decision, and our decisions
determine our direction in life, which ultimately results in
our destination. Living out our faith means we are making
decisions based on what we believe to be true. Sometimes
it is not that we choose to make a bad decision, but that

we simply do not choose to make the BEST decision. We have great intentions and we fail to take time to connect the dots between our decisions and the outcomes we will ultimately experience. Run each decision through the filter of *does that decision put you on the path to intimacy with Jesus or does it lead you astray?*

Take time to reflect on your life. Would you say you are on the path God desires for you to be walking? If you continue down this path, where will it lead? Where are you headed spiritually, relationally, financially, professionally and in every area? We can only expect to experience God's best when we walk in obedience to Him. Jeremiah 7:23 says,

> *Obey My voice, and I will be your God, and you shall be My people. And walk in all the ways that I have commanded you, that it may be well with you.*

Walking in obedience yields a blessed life and keeps our feet firmly planted on the path He has for us. His path is the only one that leads to peace and joy and blessings that abound.

Do you want to see the big picture and know where He is leading you? Me, too! I want a 5-year plan. My way wants God to shine a spotlight so I can see what lies ahead, but God tells us His word *"is a lamp to my feet and a light to my path."*[96] Visualize that. God's word is the light and it illuminates our path *one step at a time.* You see, if He were to shine the spotlight, then faith would not be required. God has already shared with us how this is going to play out. We can read the book of Revelations and learn that we will be victorious. We get the prize – eternity in heaven with Jesus! So, we know we are His and when our lives are over we will be with Him. It is the time in between when we are asked to be faithful.

Let's read Romans 1:17 together. It tells us,

For in it the righteousness of God is revealed from faith to faith; as it is written, The just shall live by faith.

What does that mean when it says from faith to faith? Well, it is by faith we are saved. Our faith was there at the beginning of our relationship with Jesus. And it is our faith that leads us home to intimacy with Him. We are to live our life by faith. Ephesians 2:8 tells us,

For by grace you have been saved through faith, and that not of yourselves; it is the gift of God, not of works, lest anyone should boast. For we are His workman-ship, created in Christ Jesus for good works, which God prepared beforehand that we should walk in them.

Our faith is not of our own doing. We cannot take credit for it and should not be prideful because of it. Our faith is a gift placed inside of us and God gets all the glory for it!

Do you know, when we are faithful we are promised the gift of God's rest? But when we demonstrate a lack of faith, we hinder our ability to receive our promised land. I have a handwritten note in my Bible near Hebrews 4 that says, I must be obedient and rest in God if I am to find my Promised Land on earth. Verse 11 tell us,

Let us therefore be diligent to enter that rest, lest anyone fall according to the same example of disobedience.

We are to be diligent to live out our faith. It is through our faith and our trust in Jesus, our belief that He is who He says He is, and our understanding that He is in control that we find rest. Anything outside of that – fear, worry, anxiety, insecurity, etc. – only brings about fretting and exhaustion.

What path are you walking and where is it leading you? We want intimacy with Jesus. Are we walking the path that will lead us there? We have a choice to make. Our salvation has secured us eternity in heaven with Jesus, but He has called us to live a life of faith. He is waiting for us to make that commitment.

This faith of ours is sure to be tested. When it is, we have an opportunity to show the world where our faith lies. When we are crushed, what attributes will we exhibit? As I raised my children I often said things like, *it is easier to do wrong than to do right. It is easier to go along with the crowd than to stand apart.* Those statements are applicable in our walk with Christ. It is easier to be distracted and skip our quiet time than to be committed to be in the Word every day. It is easier to follow the world and live as the world says is acceptable than to live a life that glorifies our Savior. It is easier to be full of fear and frustration than to be full of faith. Will we be proven faithful? Jesus came and showed us how to do that and has promised to be faithful to supply all we need.

Are you thinking about playing it safe now that you are secure in your salvation? Are you content to barely squeak into heaven? Or will you defy expectations and break out of your box? Will you be like Peter? Peter found himself in a boat in a great storm. He had a choice. He could stay in the boat and safely arrive on the other side of the sea or he could experience Jesus in a way most never will. Peter looked out on the water and he saw something. What was it? Was it a ghost? What could be out on the water in the middle of the sea? Suddenly he heard Jesus say, *"Be of good cheer! It is I; do not be afraid."* In the midst of the great storm, Peter focused on Jesus.

> *You see, when we set our sights on Jesus, lock eyes with Him and obey His command the miraculous happens.*

Imagine the two of them locking eyes. Peter said, *"Lord, if it is You, command me to come to You on the water."* Are you picturing this in your mind? Jesus said *"Come."* I imagine He stretched out His hand welcoming Peter to come to Him, and Peter did. Can you fathom it? Peter activated his faith, threw his leg over the side of the boat and stepped out onto the water. You see, when we set our sights on Jesus, lock eyes with Him and obey His command the miraculous happens. The impossible becomes possible. But suddenly Peter became aware of the strong wind and the turmoil of the sea and he lost faith, became afraid and cried out, *"Lord save me."* Do you know what Jesus did? He caught Peter as he began to sink and He said, *"O you of little faith, why did you doubt?"*[97]

As we travel this journey of living out our faith, we have a decision to make. Do we want to ride in the boat, all safe and sound or do we want to activate our faith, lock eyes with our Savior and walk on the water with Jesus? He has a plan for our lives. He wants to use each of us in ways we could never even imagine. Our answer can be, *Well, maybe...* or our answer can be one of total surrender, a faith-filled YES! Oh, I hope and pray you choose yes!

Putting it All Together

Don't you love the word "become"? Become means "begin to be." We can begin to be more like Jesus, begin doing what He is asking us to do and begin walking out our faith the way He did.

My prayer for you is that you will fall in love with Jesus, set your sights on Him, obey His commands and watch the impossible become possible. He is waiting. What will you do?

Chapter 10
What's My Purpose?

Do you know you are special? God says you are fearfully and wonderfully made.[98] He formed you, knit you together and knew you before you were in your mother's womb.[99] He made you unique with gifts and talents He desires to use.[100] God designed you and placed a call on your life. Will you heed that call and fulfill your purpose? Or will you wander around in doubt, seeing everyone else's gifts and talents, but squelching yours and denying your reason for being?

In stark contrast to God's word, we live as if we believe He created us so the world could revolve around us. We put *our* thoughts, feelings, opinions and desires on a pedestal and view everything from *our* perspective. We wallow in the way we feel about every issue and value our opinion even though it has been shaped and molded by the news media, the entertainment industry and our selfish desires. We believe we have rights and want them recognized, ignoring our responsibilities as His children. We have it all wrong.

We were not created for our self-fulfillment. Life is not all about *me*; it is about something far greater. The closer we grow in our relationship with Jesus, the more we come to understand who God is. The more we understand who He is, the more we will surrender our selfish nature to Him. The more we surrender, the more clearly we will see His plan for us, revealing His purpose and His calling for our life.

> *The more we surrender, the more clearly we will see His plan for us, revealing His purpose and His calling for our life.*

We want God to go ahead and reveal this calling. We just want to know His plan for our life. However, He is not going to reveal more to us than we are prepared to receive. So, He waits. He waits for us to do our part and grow up spiritually. You see, we start out a babe in Christ. As we grow and mature, proving our love for Him, He will entrust more of His plan to us. As we become prepared to fulfill our calling, it will be revealed. I cannot think of anything more beautiful.

This life is short. I can hardly believe I have crossed the half century mark. Shortly after my 50th birthday I picked my granddaughter up from first grade. She jumped in the car and excitedly proclaimed, "Congratulations, MeMe! You are halfway to a hundred!" I gasped and quickly protested,

"I am just as close to zero as I am to a hundred!" Her comment is funny, but the truth is - those 50 years passed quickly. Our time here is short and we cannot get back a second that has passed. If we are given more days, weeks, months or even years – what will we do with them? Will we waste them or will we surrender and allow God to qualify the unqualified, prepare the unprepared, and make possible the impossible? When will we plug in to God's plan and start making our days count for eternity.

> *Will we surrender and allow God to qualify the unqualified, prepare the unprepared, and make possible the impossible?*

We have a decision to make. Do we want our life defined by complacency or defined by our diligence to follow our Savior? Let's make our lives count. Let's leave a legacy that points others to Jesus. Let's fulfill our call.

What do we need to do to live out God's call on our life?

Well, first and foremost, we need Jesus. We must grow in our relationship with Jesus if we are to ever know and experience God's call. I know I have said that repeatedly – but it is of utmost importance. To grow, we must be honest with ourselves, recognize sin in our life and confess it. We must turn from our old ways and invite Jesus to be ruler of our lives. Will we choose to live a life that glorifies our Creator and honors our King? The only way we can is if He comes first.

Once we start growing in our relationship with Jesus, we will crave time with Him. We will want to know Him better and talk to Him more. We will want to know His desires for us. No matter where we are in our relationship with Him, we need to go deeper. Can I share a little of my story?

A few years back, I started investing more time in the Word. I studied harder, took more notes at church, got involved in a small group Bible study, started to lead a women's group, got my priorities in order and guess what? My relationship with Jesus grew. I came to know Him in a way I never had before. Spending time in God's Word will change your life.

Soon, I began hearing a whisper, *more*. What? *More*. I prayed and said, "God, I have a full plate. I work a lot, have a big family and am involved with our church. There is no 'more' of me." But still He whispered. It was overwhelming and I argued with Him. One day I stopped and simply prayed, "What do you mean *more*?" After that day, I came to understand God was not asking me to add more to my to-do list. He wanted more of me. He was calling me to grow, to change and to become more of who He created me to be.

I threw my hands in the air and agreed to do whatever He was asking me to do. From that day, I can tell you it has been an incredible journey. Scary? Yes! Overwhelming?

Yes! Easy? No! Worth it? You better believe it! It is sweet to be in communion with Jesus. Does it ebb and flow? Yes. Do I get distracted? Yes. But I am getting better at this surrender thing and letting Him have more and more of me. I encourage you to give it a try.

The next thing we need is complete trust in Him. Proverbs 3:5-6 says,

> *Trust in the Lord with all your heart, and lean not on your own understanding; in all your ways acknowledge Him, and He shall direct your paths.*

So, we are placing our trust in God and not in our ability to understand His ways. We want to be obedient to follow where He leads and wait for Him to reveal the next step.

We must trust Him because as He reveals our next step or our calling, it may not make sense to us. For example, God made it clear that He has called me to write – yet, I do not have a college degree or anything that qualifies me to write. It makes no sense to me. Writing was never a part of my plan. It is crazy and it is awesome! Mark Batterson says, "I learned that if you aren't willing to put yourself in 'this is crazy' situations, you will never experience 'this is awesome' moments." [101] I want us all to experience awesome moments where we know God is working through us and accomplishing more than we ever could have imagined.

Ephesians 3:20 says, *"Now to Him who is able to do exceedingly abundantly above all that we ask or think, according to the power that works in us."* The fact that this book is in your hands is exceedingly, abundantly above all I could have thought to ask Him to do. We can trust Him to do a great work in us, to lead us, direct us, and equip us. He does not call the qualified, He qualifies the called. You my friend are called and can do whatever He calls you to do in His strength. Trust Him to lead you to fulfill that calling. Trust Him and take a step forward.

Rest in the knowledge that no matter what – God is good! Unbelievers and young believers question "Why does this good God allow bad things to happen?" I once heard Joni Eareckson Tada offer an explanation. Joni is an Evangelical Christian author, radio host and founder of *Joni and Friends*. But that is not who she had aspired to be. As a teenager, she and her sister went to the lake for a swim. She dove into shallow water and her life forever changed. She became a quadriplegic, but God had a plan. She has allowed God to use her injury, her disabilities, and her struggles for good in her life and in the lives of others. Joni says, "God permits what He hates so that He might accomplish what He loves." Now that changes our perspective, doesn't it? The truth is Joni would not be reaching and touching the many, many thousands of lives she is today had she not endured great suffering. She impacts the lives of many thousands with disabilities, providing them wheelchairs and sharing the love of Christ.

We need to believe that God has gifted us. In I Peter 4:7-10, we read that we have been gifted to serve others for God's glory. We are expected to love, be hospitable without complaining and use our gifts. Don't say you aren't gifted – you are! Scriptures tells us about these spiritual gifts in I Corinthians 12, Romans 12 and Ephesians 4. In I Corinthians 12:7 we read, *"But the manifestation of the Spirit is given to each one [that means you] for the profit of all."* He has gifted you with gifts He desires to use for the benefit of others. In Romans, we learn that just like a body has different parts, Christians (the body of Christ) also have different parts, and we are to perform our specific function. Each Christ-follower is called to practice their God-given gifts and talents. That means no comparing and trying to be like others, but instead embracing who God created each of us to be.

What if you do not feel qualified to serve God? Well, join the club – you, my friend, are not alone. But God promised in Philippians 4:13 that we can do all things through Him who strengthens us. Ask God to reveal your gifts and how He desires to use you. Be open to taking a step when you feel led by the Lord. Instead of praying, *"God, please go with me,"* pray, *"God, help me go with You! Lead the way, Lord. Guide my steps; take me where you want me to go; show me where You want me to serve; tell me what You want me to do. I long to be with You! I do not want to step out in front of You and I don't want to lag behind. I want to walk with You, Lord! I want to walk in complete trust in You."*

We need the wisdom of God. Wisdom is not mere knowledge. Let's look at James 3:13-18,

> *Who is wise and understanding among you? Let him show by good conduct that his works are done in the*

meekness of wisdom. But if you have bitter envy and self-seeking in your hearts, do not boast and lie against the truth. This wisdom does not descend from above, but is earthly, sensual, demonic. For where envy and self-seeking exist, confusion and every evil thing are there. But the wisdom that is from above is first pure, then peaceable, gentle, willing to yield, full of mercy and good fruits, without partiality and without hypocrisy. Now the fruit of righteousness is sown in peace by those who make peace.

Wisdom that comes from above produces meekness and peace. It allows for the Holy Spirit to work in us and for us to understand that *our gifts and our blessing are from God* and not because we are wise. We are not the ones to be praised, God is. And if we have envy of others and are self-seeking, then James tell us this is demonic and will only bring about confusion. *What?* That is a hard pill to swallow, isn't it? Demonic forces influence us? Our only defense is God's truth. It can cut through and discern what is from above and what is from Satan.

Wisdom is a lifelong pursuit. We may be smart, but what we want is to activate the wisdom that can only come from above. James 1:5 says, *"If any of you lacks wisdom, let him ask of God, who gives to all liberally and without reproach, and it will be given to him."* We can pray and ask for wisdom and discernment. To live out our calling we need insight from above and confidence that God is controlling our circumstances.

Lastly, we need a willing spirit. Please don't just rush past that sentence. Pause and ask yourself this very important question. Am I *willing*? Christine Caine says "The Christian life is no spectator sport." [102] Are you spectating or are you in the game? Let God be your coach and play to your full capacity. Christine goes on to say, "He does not ask, 'Are you capable?' He asks, 'Are you willing?'" Are you willing to live out the purpose for which you were created?

So here is my suggestion. Get alone with Jesus, raise your hands in surrender and simply whisper, *yes*. Most of us are negative by nature and find it easier to say no than yes. But we should stop being negative and allowing fear and doubt to control our lives. Discovering our calling requires we say "yes" to Jesus! Not yes to every good thing that comes our way, but yes to His purpose for our life. We need our relationship with Him, our belief and His wisdom to guide our willingness so we do what He is calling us to do.

As you grow and willingly surrender to your calling, you will find He will affirm and confirm your steps through His word. He may place people in your life who will speak His truth to you. You may find certain scriptures begin to stand out. *Write them down.* You may hear a sermon and feel like the pastor is speaking directly to you. *Take good notes.* You may hear a song and be moved to tears. *Take notice.* Be willing to receive God's direction for your life. And when He prompts you to take a step – then step.

To fulfill the purpose God has created us to fulfill we must understand that we need a deep connection to our Lord and Savior. We must completely trust Him and know that no matter what, He is good! We can rest in the fact that He has given us gifts He desires to use and will supply His wisdom when we ask for it. And we must surrender and be willing to walk the path He has prepared for us so we can live out His calling on our life. But before we end this chapter, can I offer just a bit of caution?

Cautiously Consider...

Not everyone you love will understand your desire to pursue God's calling on your life. Some may be more comfortable keeping you in your box and not know what to do with you when you start stepping outside of it. God will work out the details; let Him guide you through it. You might consider being selective regarding who you talk to about your purpose. You see, people love to give their opinion, but we do not want their limited opinion, we want God's unlimited will for us. Carefully choose those who are spiritually mature and will pray with you and encourage you to understand God's will and direction for your life.

At times, the way you need to walk is clear and you feel deeply connected to Jesus. You feel His presence and His guidance. Other times, all you hear are crickets. During those times ask yourself, *Do I need to wait on Him or is He waiting on me?* Let me tell you a funny story. After I stepped out in obedience and started writing what would ultimately become this book, I became overwhelmed and filled with insecurity. I had no idea what I was doing, felt awkward and out of my element – so I stopped writing. No explanation. I just stopped. Shortly afterwards, I began to wonder, *where are you, God? Where did you go?* I had lost that intimate connection and only heard silence.

I was leading a group through one of Beth Moore's Bible studies when she began talking about this and said (and I paraphrase), "You know you have a calling and God has given you something specific to do, but you have stopped. You are wondering where God went. Well girlfriend, He is waiting on you to do what He has given you to do." Whoa! I almost fell off the couch. It was as if that video series was made just for me. Point made. I started writing again and - you guessed it - starting hearing God more clearly than ever. God had been waiting on me. When you are sure of what God wants you to do but are not doing it, He waits.

We should trust God's timing is perfect. He is never late and never early. Psalm 37:7 tells us, *"Rest in the Lord and wait patiently for Him."* As we wait patiently, we never know what work God is doing. There may be things He is working out and will reveal to us in time. He may be doing a work in us before we are ready for the next step. Maybe He is waiting for us to surrender that other part of our life, the part we are holding back because we do not believe it has anything to do with our relationship with Christ. He wants *all* of us! We are to lay our lives down the same way Jesus laid His life down for us. We are to surrender our all.

Something to Ponder

To understand our specific calling, we have to determine a few things…

1. What are your gifts? We often think of gifts as singing or speaking, but they could be things like organizing, planning, relating to others, encouraging, etc. Pray and ask God to reveal your gifts to you and help you use them for His glory. (Jot them down here.)

_____

_____

_____

_____

_____

_____

2. Who are you called to serve? Do you gravitate toward children, women or the elderly? Are you burdened for the lost, the fatherless, homeless, teenage moms or those with addictions? Do you feel compelled to share the gospel or to disciple believers? Often our burden is tied to our calling. (Write down what comes to mind.)

_____

_____

_____

_____

_____

3. What are your proficiencies? In what area do you excel? What can you do to serve and allow God to use you?

_____

_____

_____

_____

_____

Chapter 11

Sharing My Faith

We were at a business retreat. The speaker was one of the most influential people in my life - Andy Horner, the founder of Premier Designs, Inc., a direct sales jewelry business. Andy will do whatever he feels God is leading him to do. So, it was no surprise to me that in the middle of speaking to our group, he broke out into song. He began to sing, *"It is no secret what God can do. What he's done for others He will do for you."* As he sang, he pointed toward a few in the crowd then returned to his topic and closed out the meeting.

As I excused my way through the people, my friend Brittany stopped me and said, "Not right now, but after the meeting can we talk? I want to know more about what Andy was singing about." As her voice cracked and she fought back tears, she knew she needed what Andy had - that confidence in knowing he was God's and God was his.

That weekend I had the opportunity to share the plan of salvation with three friends. I never imagined I would share with even one. We were on a business-building retreat and my mind was focused on helping those who had a desire to grow their business. God's plan was bigger. He was doing exceedingly, abundantly above all I could have imagined.

As I look back, it gives me chills to recall how God brought this about. I share this because it will happen in your life as well. God will orchestrate opportunities and prompt you to do things. He will place people in your path. We must stay in the Word so our senses remain sharp and we will recognize these promptings.

The three ladies who prayed to receive Jesus were not planning to attend the retreat. I had noticed Brittany's name was not on the list of attendees. She had expressed a desire to grow her business, so I wondered why she was not attending. I felt a prompting to call her, even though I was finalizing the details. I gave her a quick call and learned she was not coming due to the travel expenses. I told her I understood and we would miss her. Later she called back and said she and her husband had decided she should attend.

As I lined up the speakers for this event, I was excited Theresa was joining us. She was driving alone from Louisiana. As we talked about her training topics and retreat details, I suggested she fill her car with some of her jewelers and have them join us for the retreat. She did. One of those passengers returned home changed, with Jesus as her Savior.

There are lots of details when you plan an event. There were more attendees flying in than driving, which meant I had a transportation problem. I called a local jeweler and asked if she would help by transporting some of the attendees. She agreed. I had no idea she had decided to not attend, but when I asked for help, she hated to say no. As we sat on the couch and she prayed to receive Jesus, through broken sobs she whispered, "This is why I am here. God brought me here for this."

Can I be real? Sitting with my Bible and leading someone to the Lord is not the norm for me, though I wish it were. It was overwhelming and all I could do was silently plead, "Lord help me. Please speak through me." Thankfully, I had my Bible with me and a note that listed the scriptures to read with someone when sharing the plan of salvation.

Remember, we talked about being *willing*. So, let me ask you, are you *willing* to share Jesus with others? Are you *willing* to be prepared for whenever the opportunity may arise? Are you willing to be brave and do it afraid, trusting God to speak through you? Are you willing to offer others the greatest gift they will ever receive? You *can* do this because of the One who lives in you. This walk of faith is not about having confidence in yourself, it is all about having confidence in God and living your life out loud in His strength. Ready?

Share Your Faith by the Way you Live

Today is a great day to start sharing your faith. We can share our faith simply by the way we live our everyday life. People are watching. Our daily activities, decisions, attitudes, responses and behaviors make it clear what we believe. When we live out our faith, people take notice. They notice the calm amid a storm and are wowed by the peace that makes no sense to them. They wonder why you are not worried, angry or bitter and are attracted to your kindness. So, become aware of what you are presenting to the world, become painfully aware.

If we realize we are not living a faith-filled life, how do we change? Well, we just wake up in the morning a brand new awesome person. It is that easy, right? No! Sorry, I can be a little sarcastic sometimes. (*wink) You know the answer, don't you? We must spend time with Jesus so He can do some transforming. Getting to know Him changes us. On our own, we are powerless to do anything. But He is all powerful and there is nothing He cannot do – even change messed up people like you and me.

The way we live out our faith used to be a walking testimony to dozens, maybe hundreds. However, these days the way we live touches thousands. Who would have ever imagined people on the other side of the planet would know what we are cooking for dinner? We are testifying to the world who we are and what we believe every single time we post on social media. We put it all out there for everyone to see. Have you ever noticed some people profess to love the Lord, but their spewed opinions, judgments of others, all-out rants and racy photos depict the contrary? What do your posts say about you?

We must be careful how we live if we want our life to reflect our Heavenly Father. Do we gossip, react angrily, have road rage, and live a sin-filled life? Are we active in the church body? Are we serving somewhere? The only cure is to pray and ask God daily, *"Lord, please help me respond to people how You would respond. Please help me love with Your unconditional love and offer grace because You gave me grace. Help me live how You are calling me to live. Make my life a living testimony that brings honor to Your name and points others to You."*

Post John 13:34-35 on your bathroom mirror. Jesus is speaking,

> *A new commandment I give to you, that you love one another; as I have loved you, that you also love one another. By this all will know that you are My disciples, if you have love for one another.*

I am not asking you to pretend to be someone you simply aren't; I am encouraging you to become who God desires you to be. He has big plans for you. There are people who will come to know the Lord because God will use your faithfulness to point others to Him.

Let your life be a living testament to how good God is. Living a life that glorifies Christ will enrich your life and the lives of others. You may be the only Bible they ever read and the only example of Jesus they ever see. Be careful, you never know who is watching you! I have a friend who shared with me that at the age of 35, she had never attended a church service. She had never heard or understood much about Jesus. Her first glimpse of who He was happened because she became friends with a few Christians who loved

Jesus out loud. Live your life in a way that doesn't show others how great you are, but how great the One alive in you is. When you do that, God will use your life and your testimony to draw people closer to Him. That, my friend, is what this life is all about.

Be Prepared to Share the Plan of Salvation

Prepare yourself to share the gospel because you never know when the opportunity will arise. How can you prepare? You can put a list of scripture to share in your Bible and in the Notes section of your phone. Don't worry about what you should say, the scriptures will do the talking for you. You can simply ask, "Do you mind if I share a few scriptures with you? They might help you the way they helped me." Once they say yes – read a scripture or two and then ask, "What does that say to you?" Read another one or two and ask the same question again.

Visit www.pampegram.com for a downloadable file with a list of scriptures to share. Prepare now to share Jesus, because you never know when you will have an opportunity to tell someone about Him. The most loving thing you can ever do is share Jesus with others. Our love for others and His love alive in us can cover our lack of knowledge or inexperience sharing Him.

Is all this talk about sharing your faith freaking you out just a little? It's okay. I totally get it. We never want anyone to think we are weird or self-righteous or a zealous fanatic. So, rest assured you do not have to force your faith on anyone. When we first accept Jesus, we want to run out and tell everybody. We want them to experience what we have experienced, but they just stare at us as if we are an alien. It doesn't take long until we feel totally awkward and ill-prepared. It's okay. Each person must come to their own realization that they need Jesus, but we may be able to inspire that realization to come a little sooner.

Prayer will prepare you. Begin praying that God will use you and your life as a living testimony to who He is. Ask God to change you, to transform you from the inside out into who He is calling you to be, so others would see Him in you. Ask God to make you sensitive to those who need Him, to give you the words to say, to control the tone of your voice and to help you share humbly – simply inviting them to learn more.

Be Brave, but Gentle

There is a happy medium between saying nothing and vomiting our religion all over people. We want to be brave and share our faith, yet be gentle with our words, making sure they are pointing others to Christ – not repelling them. We can begin to be open and share what God is doing in our lives – not in a braggadocio, 'look at me' kind of way - but in a humble, 'I am in awe of God and His goodness' kind of way. Tell your story of what God has done in your life, paying attention to their response. Continue if they show interest and cut it short if they do not. If you aren't sure, ask them, "Can I share more?" If they are asking you questions, keep going. Be brave, but gentle.

We can share our faith by offering to pray for others. People share their problems freely. A checkout clerk will tell you she is having a bad day. Ask, "How can I pray for you?" A friend cannot wait to tell you the terrible things that have happened since you last talked. Tell her, "I will be praying for you." When friends post on social media the hard situations they are walking through, reach out and let them know you are committed to pray alongside them. Prayer changes things; it makes a difference. Be brave and let others know you will pray for them and then do it. You might want to start a prayer journal and jot down notes so you don't forget to pray for those you promised you would.

I am not sure why people are so shy about praying out loud, but it is a real fear for many. Are you comfortable praying out loud with a friend? If not, will you ask yourself why? I have seen the effect it has on someone when they realize you care enough about them to pray right there, right then. It blesses them so much. Ask God to make you brave. Don't forget you have the Holy Spirit, the Living God alive in you. Call on Him and He will make you brave, giving you the courage you need to minister to others. It does not have to be an eloquent or super-spiritual prayer. Just say something like, "Jesus, I know you know the pain my friend is in. She is going through a hard time. I pray you will be with her and comfort her, Lord. Please guide her through this situation. This I ask in your most precious name. Amen." There are so many people who have never experienced someone praying for them. It will touch them, even if they are not brave enough to tell you it did.

Sharing our faith is one of the most selfless things we can do. It is proof that we love others enough to step out of our comfort zone. You see, we start out so spiritually immature that when given the opportunity to share, we immediately start thinking about ourselves. We forget there is

> *Sharing our faith is one of the most selfless things we can do.*

a person standing there who will spend eternity in hell if no one steps up and shares Jesus with them. As we grow spiritually, Jesus increases and we decrease. We learn to stop putting ourselves first, and put Him first. Should we shudder in fear or speak up in faith?

Growing closer to Jesus makes us more sensitive to the needs of others and not so sensitive to our own feelings and fears. We learn to listen to others instead of constantly talking about ourselves. People will find that refreshing and it will draw them to you. It shows you truly care. Every person has the innate need to be accepted, heard and treated as if they are important. Once people know they can trust you and that you care about them, they are more likely to be open to you sharing Jesus with them.

The quickest way to turn people away from you is if you become offended or resentful if they do not want to hear about your faith. It is okay. God calls us to share – we are not in control of the results. God has given us all free will, so someone can cling to unbelief if they choose. But you keep living a life that is a testimony to God's goodness.

Continue to love others unconditionally. Keep offering to pray for them and with them. Keep doing what God purposes in your heart to do. Be brave, but gentle. You never know when they just might come back and ask you to tell them about Jesus or agree to go to church with you.

That is what happened with Brittany. Remember my friend who accepted Jesus at our business retreat? My husband and I sat down and shared the plan of salvation with Brittany. She prayed the sweetest prayer asking for forgiveness for her sins and inviting Jesus into her heart. She returned home excited about her conversion, but worried by her husband's response to it. He was not as excited as she had hoped. She knew they needed to be in church, but he was not interested in going. So, she went alone. She bought a Bible and began to study it. She started taking steps to grow in this newfound faith. Brittany and I were together about 6 months later and she was burdened. She wanted her husband to have what she had and was hurt that he just did not get it. She was desperate to do something, anything. We prayed for him. She kept inviting him to church and stopped being offended when he did not go. A few months later I received a phone call from Brittany, excitedly sharing that Chris was going to church with her. As she prepared to make her public profession of faith by being baptized, he prayed and asked Jesus into his heart. They were baptized together.

Others notice when there is true change within us. They are intrigued by it, but do not want to be pressured into anything. So, we should give them space and time to make their decision. We just keep praying for them and asking God to put the right words in our mouth and help us to be obedient to say and do what He is calling us to. Brittany is one life transformed by her realization that she needed Jesus. God used her transformation to bring Chris to that same realization. As she has grown in her faith, she has allowed God to use her in the lives of others and she is sharing her faith with them. She and Chris are raising their son in a Christian home and teaching him about Jesus. The effects are far-reaching and who knows how God will use this one life, this one testimony to make a difference that will last for all eternity.

I Peter 3:15 (ESV) –
But in your hearts honor Christ the Lord as holy, always being prepared to make a defense to anyone who asks you for a reason for the hope that is within you; yet do it with gentleness and respect.

We share because we want to be obedient to our Lord and Savior. We share because we want others to have this priceless gift we have received. We share because them going to hell is scarier than us opening our mouths, even if we stutter and hyperventilate. We share because we love Him and we love others. We share because not sharing is costlier than risking rejection. We share because when we step out in faith, He will be faithful to be with us.

Something to Do

Be prepared to share Jesus when the moment arises. Be sure to visit www.pampegram.com and download the tools provided there. I encourage you to prepare your Bible so you can share the verses easily and have the verses in your phone – just in case. Most importantly pray and ask God to prepare you and make you sensitive to those who need Him. Ask Him to make you brave.

Who do you know who needs to know Jesus? Make a list and pray for them.

_____

_____

_____

_____

_____

_____

_____

_____

_____

Chapter 12

Time to Grow Up

Who remembers our goal? Ooh! Ooh! I do! Our goal is intimacy with Jesus. Are you ready? Are you ready to be so deeply connected to Him that you feel and experience His presence? When I was growing up, my mom used to sing hymns as she did the dishes. I remember hearing the words, *And He walks with me and He talks with me and He tells me I am His own. And the joy we share as we tarry there, none other has ever known.*[103] We want to be One with Jesus. We want to have unity with Him. There's nothing like it!

This type of connection requires that we grow up and become spiritually mature. *Spiritually mature?* Just the word "maturity" evokes all kinds of feelings in us. It doesn't sound exciting. Remember the girl in school the teacher used as an example of how maturely we should behave? She seemed bored to me and missed out on a ton of fun. I can't remember ever thinking, *oh I wish I could act mature*! And I certainly don't want to look mature, AKA *old*. Does spiritual maturity mean we should be like the old grouchy man at church who never smiles, wears a suit, and fusses at everybody? Who wants to emulate that? Well, I have good news! That is not what spiritual maturity looks like.

Spiritual maturity looks like Jesus. It exudes agape love for God and for people and it exudes grace upon grace. Spiritual maturity encompasses the fruits of the Spirit and brings about peace that passes understanding because our trust – no matter the situation – is grounded and securely rooted in our undeniable faith, unwavering belief, and complete surrender to our Lord and Savior. We can walk with Him and talk with Him, knowing we are secure.

Once we accept Jesus as our Savior we are to enter the process of growing – or maturing – and becoming more like Jesus Christ. But where do we start? Well, we start at the beginning – at the point of our salvation.

We come to Jesus as a babe, as a new creation in Christ. If a new baby is left alone, they will not grow physically or emotionally. They have needs that must be met for them to advance. As baby Christians, we have needs that must be met if we are to grow. 1 Peter 2:1-3 says,

Therefore, laying aside all malice, all deceit, hypocrisy, envy, and all evil speaking, as newborn babes, desire the pure milk of the word, that you may grow thereby, if indeed you have tasted that the Lord is gracious.

Just like a baby must have milk, we must have God's word. If a baby only had milk every now and then he would never grow. So, we need a schedule to be fed God's word. Instead of just glossing over it, we are to study and allow it to nourish us. We are fed by reading God's word, listening to sermons, participating in a group Bible study, and by studying alone at our kitchen table.

We should *"no longer be like children tossed to and fro."*[104] You see, children are gullible and vulnerable. Who would want to take advantage of a gullible Christian? Why Satan, of course! Can I tell you something? That is exactly why I am writing this book. There are many of us who came to the realization that we needed Jesus, we accepted Him as our Savior, but never grew much past that. Instead, we wander around relationally lost. We take one step forward and three steps backward. We walk in obedience for a few days and then rebel for a month. I am not judging anyone because of it, I get it. That was me for more years than I can count and I still fight to not slip and slide back today.

I became burdened by the knowledge that so many are like me. We think we know Jesus and we fool ourselves into believing we are living for Him, when we are just living for ourselves. We think we know all we need to know, when we don't know very much. We become satisfied with milk and do not realize we crave solid food.

Do you know that is in the Bible? Hebrews 5:12-14 tells us,

For though by this time you ought to be teachers, you need someone to teach you again the first principles of the oracles of God; and you have come to need milk and not solid food. For everyone who partakes only of milk is unskilled in the word of righteousness, for he is a babe. But solid food belongs to those who are of full age, that is, those who by reason of use have their senses exercised to discern both good and evil.

Let's break that down. The *first principles* are the basic truths and by now, we should be sharing those with others. But, have we become complacent? *"You have come to need milk and not solid food."* We are being warned that it is not good if we are satisfied to just have a little milk, just recognizing the basic truths. Just like babies grow, need solid foods and must learn to chew - we are to grow, learn the basic truths and then devour the meat of God's word – going deeper and deeper until He comes to take us to our eternal home.

A litmus test for where we are in our quest for spiritual maturity is what we put first in our lives. Are we living a life geared toward reaching our goals, achieving our desires and fulfilling our needs? When we are absorbed with ourselves, there is not much room left for Jesus. You see there is a paradigm shift that must take place. We must shift from being self-absorbed to being consumed with Him.

God has supplied all the resources we need to grow in Christ. The God we serve today is the same God who parted the Red Sea, raised Lazarus from the dead and resurrected Jesus from the grave. He is alive in us and we can call on Him! Because of Him, we can overcome the sinful desires of our flesh by walking step-by-step in the power of the Holy Spirit. He is always with us.

This path to pursuing oneness with Jesus and gaining spiritual maturity is not an easy path. It is not all flowers and sunshine and skipping merrily to sit in our Savior's lap. It is not the path of least resistance. If it were, there would be no faith needed. Jesus tells us, *"The thief does not come except to steal, and to kill, and to destroy. I have come that they may have life, and that they may have it more abundantly."*[105] So, we have an adversary named Satan who wants to steal, kill and destroy our growth to intimacy with Jesus. He makes the path treacherous. He knows who you are called to become and how God can use you. He does not want God's plan for you to come to fruition. So, on this path to spiritual maturity and the abundant life, get ready to encounter obstacles and detours Satan is sure to throw in our way and keep us behaving like immature lost children.

Deception

One of Satan's most destructive tools is deception. Brace yourself because he is a master deceiver. In John 8:44, Jesus says there is no truth in Satan for he is the father of lies. He uses manipulation to twist things around and lead us astray. Satan whisper lies and we believe we need more than Jesus.

Satan loves to remind us of our failures, making us feel unworthy and insecure. He wants us to carry our shame around and be rooted in bitterness. He quietly hisses, *remember what happened to you? Remember what you did? God can't use you.* If you listen and believe Satan's lies, intimacy with Jesus will elude you. Instead, rest in God's truth. Know what God's word says and tuck it deep inside your heart.

Doubt

Satan will do all he can to cause you to be filled with doubt, instead of filled with faith. He wants you to doubt your salvation and your identity in Christ. He wants you to question what you believe, and question God's goodness. So, anytime doubt creeps up, deal with it.

I have a friend who told me she doubted her salvation for years. She would worry and think, *what if I am not saved?* She would pray the sinner's prayer again and again. Finally, one night she woke her husband up fretting over her doubts. He told her this had gone on long enough and he wanted to help her get it resolved. They slid off the bed and onto their knees. She cried out to God telling Him her insecurity and what she wanted. She wanted to surrender her life to Jesus and walk in confidence that she was secure in Him. After praying and pouring her heart out to God, she crawled back up into the bed and never doubted her salvation again.

God promises that everyone who believes in Jesus will be saved. That word *believe* means we acknowledge Jesus is God, born of a virgin, crucified for our sins, resurrected to the right hand of God and that He will come again to carry us home. That belief propels us to surrender and place our faith in Jesus. If you have placed your faith in Him and made Him Lord of your life, you can lay down your doubts and trust God. If you need to, slide onto your knees and get it settled once and for all.

Satan wants you to doubt your purpose and your worth. Remember our identity is instilled in us by our Creator because of who He is and what He has done. We were created on purpose to fulfill a purpose. God said it; that settles it.

Satan wants you to doubt God's goodness. *God is good* when things are going great and God is good when everything feels like it is falling apart. Know God! Know who He is, what He has done and how GOOD He is. Jesus said, *"Why do you call Me good? No one is good but One, that is, God."*[106] All the time, God is good!

Disbelief

Disbelief - or unbelief - can put a halt to spiritual growth. You may be thinking, *Disbelief? No way. I believe!* Do you? Do you believe the Bible is the infallible word of God? If so, why are you struggling with your identity? God has told you who you are. Why are you filled with fear? God has told you He is with you. Why are you afraid to die? Jesus promised you would be with Him for all eternity. Believe!

As I prepared to write this book, a friend shared she struggled with disbelief. She didn't believe God loved *her*. Yes, He loved everyone else, but not her. She had been keeping a secret for years and thought God could never love her. Believe!

Disbelief finds its way onto our path when we least expect it. If you find yourself facing this giant, you are not alone. In the Bible, we learn of Elijah, John the Baptist and Thomas, just to name a few, who experienced times of unbelief. It is Satan's futile attempt to detour you from the path God has called you to travel.

Discouragement

Another tool in Satan's tool belt is discouragement. Sometimes we are like Eeyore, Winnie the Pooh's friend. He was gloomy, pessimistic, and could spot the negative a mile away. He was focused on what was wrong, totally missing all that was good and right in his world. What about you? Are you focused on what is wrong?

Here we are on this quest to intimacy with Jesus. Where should our focus be? Should we zoom in on one problem we have and let it completely overwhelm us? Or should we focus on our countless blessings and the truth of how good God is? Someone just thought, *Well, actually I have three problems.* To whom I would reply, *"Okay, Eeyore. Count your blessings!"*

Seriously, this is not cartoon material, this is a real-life drama. We cannot afford to waste our life worrying and whining. We have been called to walk in faith and *worry* is simply the lack of *faith.* (Ouch!) God has promised to use everything we endure – both good and bad – for good in our life.[107] Listen, we have been s*aved by grace, bought with the blood of Jesus, rescued from the depths of hell and promised eternity in heaven with Jesus!* Now, we are to live as if we believe that! We have so much to not only be thankful for, but to be excited about. Let's live like we believe it!

Distraction

Satan is cunning and has an arsenal of weapons to use to distract us. You see, he doesn't have to make us do bad things, he only needs to distract us from doing God's will. He will use…

- the television, social media, sports, friends, family, our to-do list, hobbies, ambition, laziness, the broken toaster, etc. to thwart our plan to spend time with Jesus.

- our little "g" gods to prevent us from worshipping the One True King.

- the need to please people to prevent us from pleasing God.

- our feelings to distract us from becoming who God is calling us to be.

- the longing to be a part of the crowd, to distract us from being set apart.

- the whispers of Satan's lies to distract us from God's truth.

- our need to be happy to distract us from experiencing unspeakable joy.

- the need of instant gratification so we will not wait for God to answer our prayer.

- our shame to make us want to hide from God.

- our desire to be in control to thwart our trust in Him.

God is not a God of confusion. His way is a committed and focused way. He never tries to distract us or confuse us. He tells us the truth and asks that we walk in it. Stop living distracted! The antidote is God's word. The more time we spend there, the more focused and committed we will become.

Defeat

Satan will use defeat to try to convince you to give up. He doesn't want God to use your story to make a difference for His kingdom. Have you even stopped to think that the more broken you are, the more His light can shine through you?

When I was 24 and going through my first divorce, a woman from church came to see me. She had no idea the reality of my situation, yet she told me if I went forward with my decision God would never be able to use me. I sat stunned. I felt so alone during that time and could have used some prayers. Yet, her proclamation left me feeling judged and defeated.

I am not sure why she believed that. As a matter of fact, Moses struggled with his belief and questioned God. David committed adultery. Jacob was a liar. John was self-righteous. Jeremiah was depressed. Peter denied Jesus three times. Yet, God turned their lives around and used each of them in powerful ways. No doubt, I had stepped outside of God's will and onto the wrong path. But the truth is God is a redeeming God and can use our mess-ups to change us and grow us. He can rewrite our story into a beautiful story of transformation. (Lady, if you read this, I forgive you.)

We are sure to mess up. We are sure to let our self-centeredness get the best of us or to react in an unflattering way from time to time. However, I have good news. We are not defeated! God's grace pours down like rain. All we need to do is ask for forgiveness and He washes you white as snow. The fact that you are holding in your hand a book written by someone who has messed up as much as me is a testament of God's restoring powers. He can heal your brokenness and restore your soul. Lamentations 3:22-24 says,

> *Through the Lord's mercies we are not consumed, because His compassions fail not. They are new every morning; Great is Your faithfulness. 'The Lord is my portion,' says my soul, 'therefore I hope in Him!'*

Delay

Ready for the last obstacle or road block we are going to talk about? I cannot end this chapter without talking about delay. You see, we can read this book and realize our need for spiritual maturity, then lay it down and think we will get around to it one of these days. Maybe once the kids are grown, then we can get serious about our relationship with Jesus. Maybe once this project is completed, I can start having a quiet time. Maybe one day... Well, one day never gets here. Today is the day. No more letting Satan convince you to put this off.

Listen, if you made it this far in this book, then no doubt your heart and soul longs to know Jesus more. Then do it; know Him more! There is so much more. Do not settle for less than all He has for you. Please! Do not delay! We are not promised tomorrow and this dark world we live in needs to know about Jesus. There are people who will never know Him unless you start sharing your faith.

Spiritual maturity is a beautiful thing and it can be ours. We can grow spiritually because we are not alone; Jesus is here with us. Peter tells us in 2 Peter 1:2-4 that our knowledge of Jesus grows as we mature in our faith. This is a special kind of knowledge, one that is complete. We come to understand who He is and what He did for us on a whole new level. We become more and more aware of His presence, sense His guidance and experience growth.

He has promised that if we love and obey Him, we will have fellowship with Him and He will live within us.[108] We are promised if we behold the glory of the Lord, we will become transformed into the likeness of Jesus.[109] He promises our transformation will be proof of who He is and allow others to see Him in us.[110]

Putting It All Together

How are we to grow in Christ? By staying committed to the spiritual disciplines that the Bible reveals, studying God's word so we can walk in obedience to it, developing a rich prayer life and having communion with Jesus. Fellowshipping with believers and encouraging one another. Attending church, serving and giving of our time and our talents. And being a good steward of our blessings. When we are consistent and persistent in these things, by God's grace, we will grow up in Him.

Chapter 13
Going to Battle

Does living our life committed to Jesus mean our life will be easy from this point forward? No. As a matter of fact, we are sure to experience times of trouble. Jesus said, *"In the world you will have tribulation; but be of good cheer, I have overcome the world."*[111] He did not say "some of you" or "might have." He said, *"you will have tribulation."* But then He went on and encouraged us to be of good cheer. That means we can be confident and courageous because our trust is in Him and He has *"overcome the world."*

You see, He is our strength and our security. We can trust God to see us through whatever difficulty we encounter. He has given us the gift of the Holy Spirit to counsel us, lead us and pray for us when we have

> *We can be confident and courageous because our trust is in Him and He has "overcome the world."*

no words. He has given us Jesus who is the Prince of Peace and the Seal that deems us secure. Yes, we will have times of suffering and hardship, but we have all we need to persevere and experience victory.

The feeling of security can be elusive. The world says our security here on earth is based on things other than God. We gather possessions, work hard, strive to make more money, long for the right mate, fret over our appearance, and put our faith in the money market, the new diet we found, the new career we pursue. We self-medicate with drugs and alcohol and fill our lives with friends and events, hoping it will all make us feel better. But where is this security we so desperately want, need, and crave?

God warns us about this. You see Satan wants us to be confused and focused on things that have nothing to do with putting our faith and trust in God. In I Timothy 6:10 God warns us *"money is the root of all kinds of evil."* In verse 17 He says,

> *Command those who are rich in this present age not to be haughty, nor to trust in uncertain riches but in the living God who gives us richly all things to enjoy.*

Proverbs 31:30 says,

> *Charm is deceitful and beauty is passing, but a woman who fears the Lord, she shall be praised.*

2 Timothy 2:22 tells us,

Flee also youthful lusts; but pursue righteousness, faith, love, peace with those who call on the Lord out of a pure heart.

There are many more scriptures to be listed here – but the message we are to receive is that our security is found in God and God alone. Worldly things will pass – eternal things last forever.

God calls us to be wise. We are to make smart financial decisions. We should strive to be healthy. He made us to be relational and have many friendships. None of these things are wrong, but they become problematic when we trust in them instead of trusting in God.

Remember the story when Jesus said a wise man will build his house on rock. When he talks about the Rock, He is referring to building your life on the firm foundation of a close relationship with Him. He says that if you do not build your life on Jesus, then you are foolish and your life will be built on sand. When the floods and the winds come you will not be able to withstand them. You will be washed away.[112] You see, God is a jealous God and warns we cannot serve two masters. Who is the other master? Anyone or anything we put before God. When He is the center of our lives He will lead us in how to manage our money, our relationships and every difficulty we face.

So, our insecurities are the result of our lack of faith and trust in God. Ouch! God, the creator of it all, the One who supplies the air we breathe, the One who sent His Son to die for our sins, the One who loves us so much He made a way for us to be with Him, the One who promises to never leave us, the One who has purposed us for His glory, the One who has made a place for us, the One who we will spend our eternity with – He is the One who makes us secure.

Jeremiah 17:7-8 paints a beautiful picture of security. It says,

> *Blessed is the man who trusts in the Lord, and whose hope is in the Lord. For he shall be like a tree planted by the waters, which spreads out its roots by the river, and will not fear when heat comes; but its leaf will be green, and will not be anxious in the year of drought, nor will cease from yielding fruit.*

When we place our trust in God we accrue great benefits.

When we place our trust in God we accrue great benefits. We will be made strong and our roots will run deep because we are firmly planted in Him. The heat, the drought – hard times and difficulties – will come, but we will endure those seasons and because of them bear great fruit for Him.

God has paved the way for us to be prepared and equipped during times of tribulation. Ephesians 6:10-13 tells us,

Finally, my brethren, be strong in the Lord and in the power of His might. Put on the whole armor of God that you may be able to stand against the wiles of the devil. For we do not wrestle against flesh and blood, but against principalities, against powers, against the rulers of the darkness of this age, against spiritual hosts of wickedness in the heavenly places. Therefore, take up the whole armor of God, that you may be able to withstand in the evil day, and having done all, to stand.

We are to put on the whole armor of God. Picture that. When David was preparing to fight Goliath, Saul gave him his armor to wear, but there was a problem. Saul was big and tall and David was short and small, so Saul's armor did not fit. David knew he would not be his best in this armor and the only way He could win was to put on the full armor of God.

Can you relate? David was the last person anyone would have chosen to battle a giant. He was young. His brothers were great soldiers, but not David; he was a shepherd boy. But as a shepherd, he had skills; he could use a sling. Even Goliath was shocked to see David standing there, young and handsome with no sign of battle scars. Goliath saw his staff and asked, "Am I a dog, that you come to me with sticks?" Goliath was offended and cursed David. You know the rest of that story...David was victorious.

We are like David - young in our faith and ill-equipped. Satan mocks us and is offended when we do not retreat.

Yet, when we find our strength in our Savior, we cannot be defeated. 1 John 5:4 says,

For whatever is born of God overcomes the world. And this is the victory that has overcome the world – our faith.

Because of the One who lives in us, we can be strong in His might and in His power. Like David, we are to put on the whole armor of God as we go into any battle – great or small.

Let's look at what that means. The Bible lists six pieces of spiritual armor. Four of the pieces are mentioned specifically and two are implied.

Stand therefore, having girded your waist with truth, having put on the breastplate of righteousness, and having shod your feet with the preparation of the gospel of peace; above all, taking the shield of faith with which you will be able to quench all the fiery darts of the wicked one. And take the helmet of salvation, and the sword of the Spirit, which is the word of God.[113]

Let's take a few minutes and look at each piece.

We are to wear the **belt of truth**. God's word - the real and undefiled truth - is where we find strength. We are to gird ourselves with the truth. Gird means to get ready, fasten something on, and to surround something. We need the truth to surround us and engulf us completely. This belt of truth protects us from the damage worry and fear can bring about in our life. When we strap on the belt of truth, then true, solid, non-wavering faith is ours.

We should never falter from our belief that God's word is truth. It cannot be changed or modified to make our lives easier. We cannot pick and choose which verses to believe. As a Christian, God's word defines our belief system. When we step down off that truth there is a price to be paid. Rejecting Satan's lies and focusing on God's truth, we will find great strength, peace, and total acceptance.

The Bible tells us,

If God is for us, who can be against us?[114]

Yet in all things we are more than conquerors through Him who loved us. For I am persuaded that neither death nor life, nor angels nor principalities nor powers, nor things present nor things to come, nor height nor depth, nor any other created thing, shall be able to separate us from the love of God which is in Christ Jesus our Lord.[115]

Tighten that belt of truth and place your trust firmly in God.

Next, strap on the **breastplate of righteousness**. During biblical times the Roman soldiers wore breastplates around their bodies, protecting the front of the body and the back. They were encased in it, just as we are to be encased in God's righteousness. We all possess this righteousness because of what Jesus has done for us. *"For He made Him who knew no sin to be sin for us, that we might become the righteousness of God in Him."*[116] Jesus was blameless, yet He became our sin and died for us so we could be declared righteous and justified.

In Philippians 3:7-9 Paul addresses the fact that he had personally tried to be "good" or righteous by obeying the law. He was striving to be blameless. He writes,

> *But what things were gain to me, these I have counted loss for Christ. Yet indeed I also count all things loss for the excellence of the knowledge of Christ Jesus my Lord, for whom I have suffered the loss of all things and count them as rubbish, that I may gain Christ and be found in Him, not having my own righteousness which is from the law, but that which is through faith in Christ, the righteousness which is from God by faith.*

All the things Paul thought were important didn't matter. The value of knowing Christ surpasses everything.

In Philippians 3:10, Paul goes on to say,

> *that I may know Him and the power of His resurrection, and the fellowship of His sufferings, being conformed to His death.*

This is the transforming power we have talked about. Dying to our flesh is a daily battle, but is required if we are to wear this breastplate of righteousness.

Next, we are to be **shod with the shoes of peace**. Because of our salvation, we can have peace – peace with God,[117] peace with ourselves,[118] and with our fellow man.[119]

In Philippians 4:7, Paul says,

The peace of God, which surpasses all understanding, will guard your heart and minds through Christ Jesus.

To guard means to stand watch, to prevent, to thwart, to protect. We can experience protection from external corrupting influences. He goes on to tell us in Philippians 4:8-9,

Finally, brethren, whatever things are true, whatever things are noble, whatever things are just, whatever things are pure, whatever things are lovely, whatever things are of good report if there is any virtue and if there is anything praiseworthy—meditate on these things. The things which you learned and received and heard and saw in me, these do, and the God of peace will be with you.

Let's keep going. This armor is pretty cool stuff.

The Bible says "above all" take the **shield of faith**. The ancient Roman soldier held his shield in front of him to block the flaming arrows that would come flying his way. The arrows could not penetrate the fireproof shield, and it was his protection. The same is true for our faith. Our shield of faith will yield victory. I John 5:5 tells us,

Who is he who overcomes the world, but he who believes that Jesus is the Son of God?

No doubt, Satan will shoot fiery darts our way. What will they be? They can come in the form of hard times, financial struggles, disappointments, broken relationships, sadness, discontentment, fear, insecurity, loss of a dream and many other things that bring about despair. Fiery darts are shot our way to distract us and discourage us from walking in our faith. But it is *only* faith that can protect us.

How do we grow our faith and build it up? How do we strengthen our faith so we can ensure it is fireproof? Romans 10:7 says, *"So then faith comes by hearing, and hearing by the word of God."* Hmm…there it is again. We need to spend time in God's word daily. Are you convinced yet?

Now, top it off with the **helmet of salvation**. The Roman soldiers wore helmets that were intricately designed. They were hard and protected the soldier's head. The helmet on their head made them appear to be taller than they were and look a little more impressive. Our salvation is much like this helmet. You see, God intricately designed a way for us to experience salvation, to have hope, to have a way to spend eternity with Him. His ultimate plan is one with many parts and all artfully combined. We each play a part and each have a purpose. It is complex and difficult for us to understand. Can you imagine experiencing His full knowledge when we join Him in heaven?

Our salvation is our acknowledgement that we are in Christ and shows we are a part of His army. We are marching to His orders, obeying His commands. He is the one in charge and we are following after Him. Our helmet of salvation protects our mind. I Peter 1:13 clearly instructs us,

> *Therefore gird up the loins of your mind; be sober, and rest your hope fully upon the grace that is to be brought to you at the revelation of Jesus Christ.*

We are to keep our minds focused on serving God and living our lives for Him.

And lastly, our armor is complete with the **sword of the spirit**. We learn more about this in Hebrews 4:12,

> *For the word of God is living and powerful and sharper than any two-edged sword, piercing even to the division of soul and spirit, and of joints and marrow, and is a discerner of the thoughts and intents of the heart.*

The scriptures provide our answers. It is the truth everything will be measured against. When we need to tear down a stronghold in our lives, we should grab our sword. When we are being attacked, our sword will defend us. When you are unsure, when you are broken, when you are struggling, grab God's word. Studying God's word makes us a great warrior. It grows us, strengthens us, prepares us, fills us and guides us. Never go to battle without your sword.

However, we are never to wield this sword to manipulate others or even ourselves to get our way. Ready for a humorous break? I teach my granddaughters scripture. Recently, the three-year-old was being corrected by her mom. My daughter told her she had to listen and obey. Well, she didn't have time for a lecture; she wanted to run off and play. My daughter again told her to listen to her; she was to obey her parents. She explained to this sweet preschooler that the Bible says you are to honor and obey your mother and your father. To which my sweet angel granddaughter replied, "Well, the Bible also says *'Be kind to one another'* and you are not being very kind to me." How can we help but chuckle, right? She had a quick comeback although it was not in the right context. Our lesson here is that we want to study God's word to gain understanding and insight for our personal growth. It is a sword and can cut away the things in our lives that do not line up with scripture. However, it is not a sword for us to use to wound, judge, or manipulate others.

Let's wrap this all up by looking at verse 18 which says, *"praying always with all prayer and supplication in the Spirit..."* After all this talk about the full armor of God, Paul talks about the importance of consistent prayer. We should never enter into battle without being in tune with the Great Warrior. In Psalm 37:5-6 we read,

> *Commit your way to the Lord, trust also in Him and He shall bring it to pass. He shall bring forth your righteousness as the light, and your justice as the noonday.*

All the armor in the world is of no use without prayer. We

must cry out to God, enter battle with Him by our side and He will fulfill His promise to defend us.

By going to battle wearing the full armor of God, we can be assured of victory. It may not look like our worldly definition of victory, but we can trust God with that. We want the victory He has for us, the one our minds cannot even fathom. It is important to know that no matter what comes our way, we can go on to live a victorious life. God will use our battles for good. We will become stronger, more faithful and develop a deeper and more intimate relationship with Jesus.

A Point to Ponder

God is faithful! He will be with us in times of tribulation and we can trust Him to carry us through. We can trust in, rest on, call on, believe in and turn to the Lord and He will sustain us. What is left for us to determine is – are *we* faith-filled? When our next bout with tribulation arises, what will we do? When we are pressed, what will be revealed? Oh, how I pray it will be our unfaltering faith that will shine forth revealing where we have placed our trust.

Chapter 14
Now What?

I was sitting at my kitchen island, my laptop in front of me and struggling to get words on the page. What should I say? Why was God calling *me* to write? Was He *sure* it was a good idea to use *me*? The phone rang and I welcomed the distraction; I needed a break.

I returned to the island and to my seven-year-old grand-daughter who was staying with me that day. She had the flu and although she was starting to feel better, she was not well enough to return to school. She had been sitting at the island with me, wrapped in a blanket and doing a little writing of her own. As I sat back down, she handed me a copy of her "book she had just written." It was written in pencil on white copy paper, with the lines crooked and words misspelled. That book, those words, her message, pierced my heart. Here is exactly what she had written…

He is Enuph

Hi, What is the most important thang in your life?

Is it Barbys, family, your dog, cat?

But....... What about Him you know Jesus!

Here is a sekret. He is enuph!!!!!

He loves you. You might not think so but....

His love is ENOMES!

You can't emagen!

Just in case you cannot decipher some of the words, just in case you need to read this again, and just in case you don't get it yet, let me translate. He is enough! What is the most important thing in your life? Is it Barbies, family, your dog, cat? But, what about Him – you know, Jesus? Here is a secret, He is enough! He loves you. You might not think so, but His love is enormous! You can't imagine!

That message from this little seven-year-old still makes me cry every time I read it. Why do I cry? Let me tell you why and maybe you will realize you should be crying, too.

- Because Jesus loves me, died for me and because HE IS ENOUGH! No matter what, He is enough! Oh, I love Him so and He loves me so much! I don't deserve it and certainly have not earned it. I deserve hell. But, He loves me and He offers me grace. Because He died for me, I long to live for Him!

- Because someone I love beyond measure knows this truth and gets it and wants to share it! Living my faith out loud so my children and grandchildren can watch is the most imporant thing I will ever do. God, if they copycat me, let it look like this. Please, Jesus, help me set an example of chasing hard after You! Every day, all day, I want to pursue You! Let anyone who is following me find themselves running toward You! *Help us, Jesus! Help us live our life out loud for YOU!*

> *Let anyone who is following me find themselves running toward You!*

- Because it is good news and worthy to be shared - too big to keep to ourselves. If she can write about it, so can I. It propels me to put my fingers on the keyboard, cry out to Him and let Him speak through me! It is worth learning to ignore the people who question why I write. It is worth the red marks my editor makes, because my grammar stinks. It is worth me battling through my insecurities, engaging in war with Satan, and making sacrifices to share who He is and what He has done so somebody – even just one somebody - might come to know Him more! *Oh, Jesus, let our lives be living sacrifices for You!*

Now what? Now go live your life like you *believe* that Jesus is enough, like you know He died for you personally, like you *long* to glorify Him. Make time for Him in your day. Make room for Him in your heart. Make a way to share Him and His love with others. Now is the time! Please don't delay.

Stop Making Excuses and Make Time for Him

If you are to experience intimacy with Jesus, then spending time with Him must become a priority. All of our excuses are useless. God knows the truth. If we are not spending time with Him, then we are putting everything else in our life before Him. We can do that and miss out on developing intimacy with our Savior. Or, we can stop talking about spending time with Him and start doing it. Let's get really honest - a lot of devotionals take about 2 or 3 minutes to read and we go check *Time with Jesus* off our To Do list. Did we spend time with Him or did we just want to be religious and follow the rules? Don't deny yourself the most incredible gift you will ever receive. There is nothing like experiencing the presence of your Lord and Savior. He will walk with you and talk with you, once you start walking with Him and talking to Him.

Don't let Satan convince you that time is an issue. It is not the quantity of time, but the quality of time you spend. Devotionals are a great way to start the day, but take time to read the scriptures and talk to Jesus about what He has for you as you read. Find some time to invest in a Bible study –

alone, with your spouse, or in a group. That is a valuable way to use your time because it encourages our transformation. If you are reading His word and don't understand it – do the same thing you would tell your child to do with his algebra homework. Review, study, get a tutor or whatever it takes for you to learn and gain understanding.

Allow your communication with Jesus to grow into all day long conversations. We are to *"Rejoice always, pray without ceasing, in everything give thanks; for this is the will of God in Christ Jesus for you."*[120] Stop focusing and worrying about the things that do not matter. Rejoice because what matters is we have received the great gift of God's grace and will spend our eternity with Him. We don't have to wait until we get there. We can spend time with Him now and use our time He has given us to point others to Him. That is what matters. Do you want your children to be "A" students or is it more important they become passionate followers of Christ? Do you care your friend is difficult or that she is lost and you would be difficult, too if it weren't for the Holy Spirit alive in you? You get the idea. As you commune with Jesus, change your mindset from *What are You going to do for me today, Lord to What are* **We** *going to do today? Who can* **We** *share with? Where can* **We** *make a difference?* Walk with Jesus!

Spending time with Jesus should include singing praises to Him. Raise your hands and worship your King. (It's okay, all you pew clinchers. I used to be one, too.) We are to worship and praise our King because we are filled with gratitude. We offer up our worship and our adoration for all He has done. We get to exalt His Holy Name, because we know there will come a time when at the mention of His name, *every* knee will bow and *every* tongue will confess that Jesus Christ is Lord. We do not have to wait until *that* day or until we enter the pearly gates; we get to glorify Him today! Let the abundant life begin now and let it begin in us!

If we find ourselves at a loss for what we should be thankful for, it is because we are lost relationally. Turn around, run to Jesus and remember what He has done! We are to be thankful for our salvation. Have we forgotten we have been saved from spending our eternity in the deep pits of hell? Have we forgotten what Jesus endured for us? Are we so incredibly filled with ourselves that we have stopped being thankful? I could go on a crazy rant on this one, but you get it, right? Make time for Jesus, because you have so much to thank Him for.

Stop making excuses and make time to spend with your sweet Savior. He knows our hearts and is waiting for our hearts to long to know Him intimately. Desire it! Crave it! Savor every second you can with Him. This is our quest for the rest of our days.

Make Room in Your Heart for Jesus

Now what? Now let's make more room for Jesus! We have some rearranging to do, don't we? We have got to clear the clutter of our feelings and fears, everything we have loved more than we loved Jesus, and all our broken parts. These things are taking up too much space, space that could be occupied by Him. Jesus is to be on the throne of our hearts. He is the only One we should ever let have that place or position. Jesus first, everything and everybody is secondary to Him.

Look deep within. What is in your heart? Are you still filled with anything other than Him? Bitterness, anger, resentment, loss, heartbreak, ambition, addiction or sadness? What is in there? Go kneel at the foot of the cross, cry out to Jesus and give it to Him. He can handle it! He will deal with it for you, all you need to do is let go of it. Ephesians 3:14-20 tells us,

> *For this reason I bow my knees to the Father of our Lord Jesus Christ, from whom the whole family in heaven and earth is named, that He would grant you, according to the riches of His glory, to be strengthened with might through His Spirit in the inner man, that Christ may dwell in your hearts through faith; that you, being rooted and grounded in love, may be able to comprehend with all the saints what is the width and length and depth and height – to know the love of Christ which passes knowledge; that you may be filled with all the fullness of God. Now to Him who is able to do exceeding abundantly above all that we ask or think according to the power that works in us.*

Make room in your heart for Jesus. Be filled up with love for Him. He loves you *exceedingly abundantly above* all you could imagine. He wants to do a work in you that is *exceedingly abundantly above all* you could ever hope. He wants to use your life in ways that are *exceedingly abundantly above all* you could ever dare to dream. You my friend are loved!

> *See what great love the Father has lavished on us, that we should be called children of God! And that is what we are!* [121]

Have we forgotten already? God loved us so much He sent His only Son to die for us! We are loved lavishly! Dictionaries tell us lavishly means in a sumptuously rich, elaborate or luxurious manner.

Do you know what Jesus asks of us? He asks us to love Him, obey Him and to make our life a living sacrifice. We are to love Him with all of our being. Scripture makes it clear - if we love Jesus, we will obey Him. Anytime we stumble, lose our way and find ourselves walking in disobedience to God's word, we have a heart issue. Turn around and surrender to the One who has lavished His love on us.

Because we love Jesus, we can love others well. We can open our hearts and learn to let God's love pour out. That means we can learn to show love and respect, be kind and considerate, and forgive and let things go. The Bible tells us our love for Jesus will be apparent by how we love others. So, look within. If you have hard feelings and resentment toward others, scripture tells us,

> *We love Him because He first loved us. If someone says, 'I love God', and hates his brother he is a liar*

for he who does not love his brother whom he has seen, how can he love God whom he has not seen? [122]

People can cause us great hurt and heartbreak. But love is a choice we make – not because people have earned our love – but because we are commanded to love. We can do it because what He has done for us is greater than what anyone has done to us! Can I get an amen? Amen!

> *What He has done for us is greater than what anyone has done to us!*

So, let's make a declaration. Raise your hand to heaven and say, *"For all my days and in all my ways, I will love you, Jesus! I will draw near to you and pray my love for you grows and grows. I will rest in the love you lavish on me. I will allow it to fill me to overflowing! Because you love me, I will love others. You are enough! You are all the love I need! I will make time for You and I will make room for you. Fill my heart, Lord! You are enough for me!"*

Make a Way to Share Jesus

My greatest desire is that my life might inspire others to fall in love with Jesus. My prayer is that God has used this book to draw you closer to Him. I pray you love Jesus more today than you did yesterday. But can I remind you of something? I am not a scholar and there are so many things

I do not know and do not understand. Sometimes a friend will say, *You know in the Bible when so and so happened?* And I smile so she will continue, but in my mind, I am thinking, *I have never heard of that in my whole life.* I have been honest about my failures and insecurities and even my inadequacies, yet you have kept reading. So, let me ask you a question. All those reasons you use to not talk about Jesus or pray out loud for hurting friends or to lead a Bible study – on what are your reasons based? Who told you that? Who told you not to share Jesus with your friends, pray to Jesus on their behalf or lead them in getting to know Jesus more? We could never answer that question with *God told me,* so it must be, well who is the opposite of God – that's right, Satan.

Instead, 2 Corinthians 12:9-10 tells us,

> *And He said to me, 'My grace is sufficient for you, for My strength is made perfect in weakness.' Therefore, most gladly I will rather boast in my infirmities, that the power of Christ may rest upon me. Therefore, I take pleasure in infirmities, in reproaches, in needs, in persecutions, in distresses, for Christ's sake. For when I am weak, then I am strong.*

Do you know what that means? When we don't have the strength or ability to do what God is leading us to do, He gives us His power. We are not supposed to do it with our own strength. We are to humbly submit and wait for Him to work through us. He makes the impossible possible. And when we are willing to do it afraid because we know He will not fail us or let us down, then we experience His presence and His provision. Oh, what a beautiful experience that is. Don't miss out!

You have been saved by God's amazing grace! So, now what? Well, God is making a way to use you and your life so others will come to know Him through you. What will that look like? I don't know. What will He ask you to do? I have no idea. Where will He want you to go? Who knows? What should you be doing? You should be getting ready to answer His guidance, His direction and His call with the word, YES! Get busy falling in love with Jesus and He will tell you and show you everything you need to know right when you need to know it.

> *When we are willing to do it afraid because we know He will not fail us or let us down, then we experience His presence and His provision.*

Don't fall into the trap of comparing what God calls you to do with what He calls others to do. Be open and listen to what He has for you. He only asks us to be obedient to serve right where He wants us to serve, to speak up when He prompts us to speak up and to be willing to do whatever He asks us to do. Our desire should be to make Jesus known and for others to come to know how great He is!

There are people waiting for you to share Jesus with them! Pray and ask God to make you sensitive to those who need Him. Ask Him to make you bold, to make you brave! The last words in the book of Matthew are known as the Great Commission. In Matthew 28:19-20 Jesus says,

> *Go therefore and make disciples of all the nations, baptizing them in the name of the Father and of the Son and of the Holy Spirit, teaching them to observe all things that I have commanded you; and lo, I am with you always even to the end of the age.*

So, there you have it. Jesus said it and that is good enough for me. Allow God to make a way for you to share Jesus! Open your mouth and let God speak through you. Be His hands and feet in this lost world we live in. God will use you to touch the lives of others for eternity!

Hey, can I tell you something? I have enjoyed my time with you. I love Jesus and know Him more today than I did when I began this book. Thank you for walking this journey with me. We are friends now, so let's keep encouraging one another on our journey to intimacy with Jesus. Let's stay in touch!

Oswald Chambers said in His devotional, *My Utmost for His Highest,*

> *Once we get intimate with Jesus we are never lonely and we never lack for understanding or compassion. We can continually pour out our hearts to Him without being perceived as overly emotional or pitiful. The Christian who is truly intimate with Jesus will*

never draw attention to himself but will only show the evidence of a life where Jesus is completely in control. This is the outcome of allowing Jesus to satisfy every area of life to its depth. The picture resulting from such a life is that of the strong, calm balance that our Lord gives to those who are intimate with Him.

Now what? Go! Run! Make time for Jesus! Make room in your heart for Him! Share Him with others! Talk about what He has done and tell of His goodness. You will never get enough of Jesus, yet you will be completely satisfied! He loves you exceedingly abundantly above all you can fathom. He is all you need. He is enough! Keep going, keep growing, deeper and deeper still! He has so much He wants to share with You. Grab His hand and walk with Him!

References

Chapter 1
1. Isaiah 30:21
2. John 3:16
3. Jeremiah 29:11
4. Romans 3:24 LB Translation
5. 2 Corinthians 9:15

Chapter 2
6. 2 Corinthians 5:17
7. Psalm 68:19-20 NIV Translation
8. John 1:12
9. Ephesians 1:7
10. John 15:16
11. Colossians 2:9-10
12. Romans 8:37-39
13. Ephesians 2:10 NLT Translation
14. 1 John 3:1-3
15. Romans 8:17
16. John 10:28
17. Mark 9:23-24
18. John 10:10

Chapter 3
[19] Galatians 4:7
[20] Romans 8:15b
[21] John 14:23
[22] John 16:7
[23] Luke 12:24
[24] James 1:17
[25] Philippians 4:19
[26] Romans 6:4
[27] 2 Peter 1:4

Chapter 4
[28] Isaiah 55:9
[29] I Timothy 1:17
[30] 2 Samuel 7:22
[31] Malachi 3:6
[32] Ephesians 2:4-5
[33] Isaiah 65:16
[34] 2 Corinthians 1:3
[35] Romans 9:15
[36] Romans 5:17
[37] 1 John 1:5
[38] Acts 17:31
[39] Hebrews 12:6
[40] Galatians 3:13-14
[41] 1 John 4:10
[42] Ephesians 1:7
[43] Romans 5:10
[44] Romans 6:23
[45] John 15:13-15
[46] I Timothy 6:15
[47] John 8:12
[48] Matthew 21:42
[49] Hebrews 6:19
[50] John 1:29

51 Ephesians 1:13
52 John 16:7
53 John 16:13
54 James 1:5
55 Isaiah 30:21
56 Galatians 5:22-23

Chapter 5
57 Matthew 6:24
58 Matthew 22:37-39
59 John 13:35

Chapter 6
60 Dr. Robert Jefress – Pathway to Victory website, Daily Devotional, Feb. 20, 2015
61 Romans 8:1
62 2 Timothy 3:16-17
63 Romans 12:12
64 Matthew 5:44
65 Philippians 4:6
66 Colossians 4:2
67 Mark 1:35
68 Matthew 14:23
69 Luke 6:12
70 Matthew 6:9-13
71 James 4:3
72 James 4:15
73 Cowman, L. B. E.; Reimann, Jim (1997). *Streams in the Desert: 366 Daily Devotional Readings* (pp. 32-33). Zondervan.

Chapter 7
[74] Acts 11:19-26
[75] *Nelson's Complete Study System* – New King James version.
[76] John 13:35
[77] Luke 23:34
[78] Matthew 6:14-15
[79] Romans 12:1

Chapter 8
[80] James 4:7-8
[81] Luke 4:8b
[82] Exodus 20:3
[83] Exodus 20:5-6
[84] John 15:9-10
[85] John 15:11-12
[86] John 15:13-17
[87] Hebrews 10:24-25
[88] 2 Corinthians 9:6-8
[89] A.W. Tozer, *The Pursuit of God*

Chapter 9
[90] Cowman, L. B. E.; Reimann, Jim (1997). *Streams in the Desert: 366 Daily Devotional Readings* (pp. 81-82). Zondervan.
[91] Hebrews 11:1
[92] Ephesians 3:20
[93] Philippians 4:13
[94] Romans 8:28
[95] Philippians 4:19
[96] Psalm 119:105
[97] Matthew 14:22-33

Chapter 10
[98] Psalm 139:14
[99] Isahiah 44:24
[100] I Peter 4:10

[101] Mark Batterson, *The Circle Maker: Praying Circles Around Your Biggest Dreams and Greatest Fears.*

[102] Christine Caine, Undanted: Daring to Do What God Calls you to Do

Chapter 12

[103] *In the Garden*, Author: C. Austin Miles (1913)

[104] Ephesians 4:14

[105] John 10:10

[106] In Mark 10:18

[107] Romans 8:28

[108] John 14:23

[109] 2 Corinthians 3:18

[110] Romans 12:2

Chapter 13

[111] John 16:33b

[112] Matthew 7:24-27

[113] Ephesians 6:14-17

[114] Romans 8:31

[115] Romans 8:37-39

[116] 2 Corinthians 5:21

[117] Romans 5:1

[118] Philippians 4:7

[119] 1 Thessalonians 5:13

Chapter 14

[120] 1 Thessalonians 5:16-18

[121] I John 3:1 (NIV)

[122] I John 4:19-20

Your relationship with Jesus matters.

As you continue down the path to intimacy
with him, visit **www.pampegram.com**
for inspiration and encouragement.

Be sure to sign up to receive the *Master What Matters*
blog posts and be the first to know about new tools,
Bible studies and any exciting new announcements.

Let's stay connected.